Designing
Your Natural Home

A Practical Guide

Designing
Your Natural Home

A Practical Guide

David Pearson

COLLINS | DESIGN

An Imprint of HarperCollins*Publishers*

DESIGNING YOUR NATURAL HOME - A PRACTICAL GUIDE

HarperCollins books may be purchased for educational, business, or sales promotional use.
For information, please write: Special Markets Department, HarperCollins Publishers Inc.,
10 East 53rd Street, New York, NY 10022.

First Edition

First published in 2005 by:
Collins Design
An Imprint of HarperCollins*Publishers*
10 East 53rd Street
New York, NY 10022
Tel: (212) 207-7000
Fax: (212) 207-7654
collinsdesign@harpercollins.com
www.harpercollins.com

Distributed throughout the United States by:
HarperCollins*Publishers*
10 East 53rd Street
New York, NY 10022
Fax: (212) 207-7654

Design by Lucy Guenot

Library of Congress Control Number: 2005927869

ISBN 0-06-076143-1

Printed and bound in China
First Printing, 2005

To all the natural home
 builders who have
helped to create this
book, and for all the
natural homers of
the future.

contents

introduction

The Earthship visitor complex (right) and SunHawk (above) are both inspirational examples where people can learn about and venture into sustainable living.

You are about to embark on a journey of discovery. A journey on which you will find out about new ways of living and new approaches to designing and building your natural home. And you will not be alone. There are many people just like you setting out on similar voyages of discovery. And there are many who have already ventured forth and have lived to tell their tale. In this book you will find ten of those who have taken different personal journeys to create their own natural homes. Woven around these real-life situations you will also find sequential practical advice to act as your guide from start to finish.

Why do we need to embark on this journey? The reasons are all too evident. It is becoming ever more imperative that we live sustainable lifestyles and live in sustainable homes. The Western world has lived beyond its environmental means for decades and is continuing to use up precious, non-renewable world resources at an unsustainable rate. And while the West has still not managed to control its excesses, newer

developing nations, such as India and China, with huge growing populations are beginning economic revolutions that will inevitably bring with them further massive burdens on world resources. Fossil oil, coal, and natural gas are being consumed as if they are infinite; vast tracts of tropical rainforests are still being cleared; old wetlands are being drained; oceans are being over-fished; and wildlife is being pushed to the margins.

With this comes pollution of land, sea, and air. Of all these, the spectre of global warming threatens the most far-reaching consequences.

SunHawk's eyrie (top), wood on stone at Tesuque Econest (above), solar water heating at the Funk Homestead (right), and a rain chain at Tesuque Econest (detail opposite).

Unless emissions of greenhouse gases from human activity are significantly lowered right now, climate changes across the globe will bring extreme weather conditions that are hard to predict. We have seen these already in unusually severe storms and tornadoes. Flooding is definitely on the increase and many more homes than ever are at real risk. If the world's polar ice sheets continue to melt, sea levels will rise and many of the world's major coastal and riverside cities will become inundated. Whole island groups will disappear.

But even though the world is going to be a more difficult place to live in, it is better to be doing something to improve the situation than burying your head in the sand and carrying on as usual. Small changes can make a difference if lots of people start to make them, and you can make a difference, too. It is all a matter of lifestyle and personal choice. From the point of view of global warming, we all need to cut our "carbon footprint" and try to lead carbon neutral lifestyles. This means living in energy-efficient and non-polluting homes.

The home is where it is all about and it is the place where you can directly contribute to helping to improve the environment. Home, too, is where you can have a major impact on the other major issue of today – personal health. Chemical

Spiral House and its meditation dome (opposite), the guest den at Orchard House (left), and light and shade creates abstract imagery at Tesuque Econest (below).

pollution is present in the food we eat, in the water we drink, and in the air we breathe. Chemical sensitivity and respiratory problems, such as asthma, are on the increase and you need to know how to protect yourself and your family against these, too.

Creating and adapting your home to reduce resource impact is vital, as is action to improve the health and healing qualities of the home. The ten homes featured in this book offer a range of different objectives, lifestyle stages, budgets, approaches, and locations. Each project was selected for its particular building techniques, ecological features, size, and use, and to give a spread from urban affordability to remote, luxurious autonomy. Each personal story shows how all those involved – the owners, architects, builders, and craftspeople – faced different challenges, yet all worked together as a creative team, often experimenting with new materials and systems, to produce unique and attractive natural homes. Each learned and discovered exciting, and sometimes quite unexpected, things about themselves, their team mates, and their homes. Each found their own ways of living

more in tune with nature and with themselves. And in the end, they all grew stronger within themselves as they became wiser and more empowered by the process.

If you embark on this journey, you too will find your own way to create your natural home. And hopefully, if you follow the guidance in this book from start to finish, you will avoid some of the worst pitfalls and have a smoother, safer, and more enjoyable trip.

We can all do something. For is it not said that a journey of a thousand miles starts with a single step? So, have a wonderful journey and be sure to take that first step today!

1 POSTS STANDING

This log house, built on a tiny island off the coast of British Columbia, Canada, was inspired by Japanese temples and First Nations' long houses. Expressing a tree-like verticality, the house is built around a number of massive, de-barked tree trunks.

When a wooded, rocky waterfront site came up for sale on tiny Gambier Island, off the coast of British Columbia, Canada, Bruce Ramus and his wife Lynno, a busy creative couple, jumped at the chance of building their new home and year-round refuge there.

Ever since Bruce had been a small boy, he had wanted to live in a log cabin, but he could not see why the logs in traditional cabins were always horizontally placed. Trees were vertical, so why could not the logs in houses be vertical too?

Lynno shared Bruce's love for wooden buildings and added her own ideas in the form of a scrapbook of clippings of her favourites, ranging from the Japanese temples to First Nations' long houses. But when they searched for an architect to help them create their joint vision, most of those they approached were not encouraging.

This was until they found architect Henry Yorke Mann. Listening carefully to the couple and looking at the scrapbook, he soon suggested some main features. He noticed that most of the ceilings in the pictures were vaulted and that — just as in Japanese buildings — prominent and complex roofs were powerful influences. "I saw the house as a family of roofs," he says. This concept also expressed the diversity of inner spaces the clients wanted. Some, such as the living room and master bedroom, were to be self-contained; others, such as kitchen and dining areas, were to be open plan and free-flowing. To meet Bruce's wish for tree-like verticality, Mann designed a structure that would be supported by massive, solid-timber posts, one as big as 1.2m (4ft) in diameter. Chosen and logged individually from the plentiful local supply, the tree trunks were de-barked while still wet to give the posts their characteristic smooth, silky gold appearance. And it is the 34 western red cedar posts that give the Ramus house its remarkable character and its name — Posts Standing.

Bruce and Lynno were both keen to use a sustainable architectural approach employing only integral natural materials, as opposed to synthetic or plastic materials, for their timeless qualities,

Some of the locally sourced cedar tress trunks that support
the Ramus house and inspired its name – Posts Standing –
can be seen in this view (above). Note the concrete buttresses
positioned around the perimeter of the building and bolted to
the trunks. These provide essential seismic resistance in this
earthquake-prone area.

inherent safety and predictability, and their non-toxicity to humans and the environment. Their requests were simple: primary rooms should have natural light on at least two sides; the minimum number of trees should be felled and removed to make way for the building; and the limitations of building on an island should be respected. In addition, extra accommodation was to be planned in the form of a studio and bedroom for guests or future family.

Working with Kirk Stockner and Steve Ladner of Quantum Construction, a site for the home was selected with great care so that only one tree had to be removed. Then, as construction

Building sustainability

The builder's deep commitment to the project fostered an atmosphere of on-going communication between the parties. This allowed the house to evolve in an organic manner, with modifications proposed and discussed on all sides. The project, for financial reasons, was constructed over the course of three summers. To take account of sustainability issues, the following elements were designed into the building:

• Deep overhangs to reduce summer solar heat gain and protect the building from the elements, while permitting winter solar heat gain.
• Ample windows and careful roof positioning for morning sun penetration deep into all areas of the house.
• Post-and-beam construction with large logs and timbers to minimize energy use for timber processing and to optimize potential recycling, as compared with standard dimensions of lumber.
• Prevention of sick building syndrome through the use of "breathing" solid wood interior and exterior walls treated only with nontoxic oils.

started, the two-bedroom 185 sq m (2,000 sq ft) design was laid out and tweaked to find the best orientation. As Gambier Island is in a zone of the highest earthquake intensity, extensive reinforced concrete foundations were essential. To give extra lateral support and seismic resistance, the structural cedar posts were bolted to a series of perimeter concrete buttresses.

While the house is firmly rooted in the ground, the cascading roofs of the final design give, as Mann describes, "the impression of a fluttering thing settling on the ground". Once the roof was complete, the 15cm (6in) solid-cedar walls were erected to fill the frame — with all planks vertical, as Bruce desired. Although the

The craft-built masonry heater, made entirely from recycled materials, is the focal point of the living room (right), creating a warm and comfortable space.

timber-plank and metal-covered roof is heavily insulated, the mass provided by the walls and posts was sufficient in itself. Large, south-facing windows allow passive solar gain and a wood-burning masonry heater, purpose-built by a local mason, provides back-up heating. This is very efficient as it only needs to be lit once a day for a short time. The heat stored in the masonry is slowly released to give daylong gentle warmth. All the fireplace masonry is made of recycled brick. Water in this predominantly wet local climate is never a problem, and all household needs are supplied from a shallow, on-site well.

The thoughtful placement and management of the building minimized pollution, transportation, fuel use, and construction impact on the island itself. As there is no car ferry service, as many of the materials as possible were sourced locally. Log harvesting and timber milling, for example, were both done on the island. Concrete was hand-mixed using local aggregates, and the construction crews lived there during the building periods. The house's large supporting posts were raised manually "Egyptian-style", says Bruce.

ecodata

CONSTRUCTION
- Log posts and timber beams
- Deep concrete foundations with anchor buttresses
- Metal roofing laid on timber planking with insulation

MATERIALS
- Local western red cedar
- Local craftspeople employed
- Metal roof on insulated cedar deck
- Ceramic floor tiles

SOFT ENERGY SYSTEM
- Photovoltaic system not ideal in overcast coastal climate

HEATING
- Good insulation reduces heating need
- Wood-burning masonry heater

COOLING
- Shading by forest trees
- Natural ventilation
- Vaulted ceilings help to vent warm air
- Roof overhangs provide shade from summer sun

WATER
- Shallow well

LANDSCAPE
- Minimal disturbance to site

Only the largest of them needed a local island contractor's logging crane to lift it into place.

As challenging as the house was to build, in the end it looks and feels simple. The natural, unpainted materials, exposed grey concrete, posts, vaulted ceilings, and natural light all blend to make the house a haven of peace and serenity.

Mann's philosophy is that architecture reflects the spirit or soul and that it should combine with reverence the practical and spiritual needs of the owner, together with a healthy respect for the site. "Listen to the client and listen to the site" advises Mann. The intent of the design, he feels, is summed up in the words of author Robert McCarter, when writing of Frank Lloyd Wright: "… to endeavour to make present the ancient understanding of building as a sacred act and buildings as sacred spaces". Mann stresses that a building should evolve as a growing process – a partnership between client, architect, contractor, and crew. If this principle is followed, without the architect's ego being involved, he promises that the result will be richer and more satisfying – it is all about working, he says, with "a common heart and purpose".

The circular, Japanese-inspired door and simple lines (above and above left) express the architect's love of sacred space.

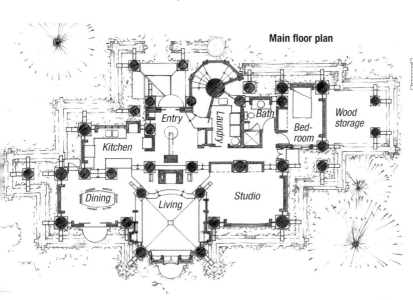

Main floor plan

Upper floor master suite

design for natural living

In harmony with nature (above), the healing window seat at Orchard House.

The grotto of the Jameos del Agua, Lanzarote, was César Manrique's first construction (opposite), open to the sky and at one with all the elements.

Designing for a natural lifestyle

Before you start designing and building your natural home, you need to be aware of some basic guiding principles and concepts.

Three powerful themes will recur as you choose your approach. These are ecology (*is your home sustainable?*); health (*is your home safe and healthy?*); and spirit (*does your home feel harmonious and welcoming?*).

A natural home needs to include and balance these aspects so that one does not dominate or exclude the others. A sustainable and energy-saving home that uses toxic materials will not be a healthy home. A healthy home that is not properly insulated or uses materials from an endangered source will not be a sustainable home. And, a home that is strong on personal and spiritual harmony yet is built of harmful materials and uses energy-hungry appliances is neither healthy nor sustainable.

The concept of Gaia sees our planet as a living organism and, like the ancient Greek earth-mother goddess, she is always seeking to create and sustain life. To be in harmony with Gaia, our homes need to be microcosms of her planetary systems and draw inspiration from her life-sustaining, healing, and spiritual dimensions.

Sustainable design

The three Rs – Reduce, Reuse, Recycle – have become the watchwords for green living and sustainable design. They are easy to remember and vital to practise when you design, build, and maintain your natural home.

Reduce

Living in and building smaller (but not cramped) homes, and building more compactly in the form of well-designed terrace (row) housing and apartment blocks are important as these reduce the "footprint" of your house on the land. This, in turn, means your home needs less of everything: less building materials, less furniture, less heating, less lighting, and less things to go wrong! Try, too, to embody proximity in the location of your home – living close to work, school, stores, health, and leisure facilities reduces time-wasting, stressful and costly commuting, and travel. Be

environmentally friendly and help reduce fuel consumption, pollution, and noise (see pp. 40, 76, and 81).

Another way to reduce environmental impact is to design or adapt your home to work with nature so that it is sheltered and makes best use of the free energy from sun, wind, and water. At one extreme, you can live off-grid by incorporating passive solar heating and cooling, photovoltaics, solar water heating, plus wind and hydro power (see pp. 28–33, 64–9, and 134–9). But if you are not able to go this far, you can still make changes, such as the options in the box below, which range from nil cost to fairly expensive.

Reuse

Another way to limit the environmental impact of your home is by avoiding new materials and products as far as possible. Search instead for used building materials, such as doors, windows,

- Switch off televisions and computers when they are not in use and do not leave them on standby.

- Turn off lights when rooms are not in use.

- Draught-proof windows and doors.

- Replace wasteful incandescent light bulbs with low-energy compact fluorescents.

- Fit and turn down heating thermostats.

- Lag all water pipes and fit an insulation jacket to your hot-water cylinder.

- Use energy-efficient kitchen appliances.

- Insulate any loft space.

- Insulate external walls.

- Fit double-glazing or low-emissivity windows.

NB: Some of these may qualify for government grants or assistance, especially for the elderly and infirm.

Collected cans and bottles (left) ready for reuse as building materials in one of the Earthships.

Seen from any angle, an Earthship (opposite) blends into the landscape.

The final effect (below), a wall built of cans and bottles.

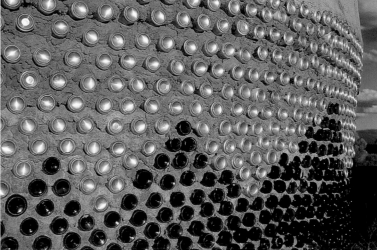

beams, tiles, flooring, panelling, and even stained glass, bathtubs and wash basins. Ask friends or contact local demolition contractors, architectural salvage, and reclaimed materials companies (or look on the web, see pp. 152–5). You can find almost anything you want – from old oak beams from a farm barn, an entire wood-block floor from an old church, or ornamental panelling from a former town hall, to a stained-glass window from an Art Deco hotel. And, with a little time, you may find enough wood to build all the cabinets in your house from a local unwanted wine vat (see pp.134–9). Even used car parts, such as hatch-back windows and doors, can find unexpected and stylish uses in the home (see pp. 76–81).

In fact, found items can be so surprising that they inspire you to modify your designs to accommodate them. However, unless you are lucky, items like this do not usually come cheap. In addition, making used items ready for reuse can sometimes be quite a task and may be expensive if put out to a contractor.

Such time-consuming jobs as cleaning and de-nailing timber beams and floorboards, removing broken glass and reglazing old window frames, and stripping thickly encrusted paint from wood or plaster mouldings fall more into the category of "labours of love" rather than regular building work. However, reused items are generally more than worth the extra time and cost, and they certainly add interest, individuality, and value to your home.

Recycling

Every time you use recycled materials instead of new, you lessen the load on the environment. New products have "embodied energy". This is the energy that is used "cradle to grave" – from extraction to manufacture, distribution, and finally to disposal. Some products, such as aluminium or cement, have very high embodied energy. So by using recycled products you make a second or third use of this original energy, instead of incurring new energy by using new products.

Use recycled-content materials. For example, cellulose insulation made from recycled paper or waste wood chips are good for both roof and wall insulation. Used car tyres, when filled with rammed earth, make strong, load-bearing walls for Earthships, while glass bottles and aluminium cans serve as ideal "bricks" and decoration for internal partitions (see p. 103). Rubber from tyres also makes excellent roof tiles that look just like slate and have the advantage of not being brittle (see p. 136). Recycled plastics offer other possibilities from garden furniture to textiles, rugs and carpets. However, with indoor products take a test sample home to see if there is a problem with off-gassing or unpleasant chemical smells before you decide. Some people may be allergic to certain artificial chemicals in these recycled products. Also look for products with sustainable disposal potential – preferably ones that are biodegradable or even capable of being demountable and taken apart for reuse rather than being consigned to the dump. And finally, try to source locally. This is not only more convenient for you, it also helps boost local business and, once again, saves on pollution and transport.

Healthy design

Along with keeping your environmental footprint as light as possible, which is often referred to as "treading lightly", you need to make sure that you live in a healthy home.

Everyone is aware of atmospheric pollution, but most people do not usually associate it with the insides of their homes. But when German and Swedish researchers first found that indoor pollution levels could be many times higher than the air outside the home, they launched a new "healthy home" movement.

The main culprit was found to be pollution arising from the dramatic increase in the use of artificial chemicals and additives in almost every product in the home. They are now endemic and range from common synthetic consumer products, such as chemical cleaners, polishes, and insect pesticides, to artificial textiles and carpets, foam-filled upholstery, vinyl flooring, petrochemical paint, and formaldehyde-containing building boards, chemically treated timber, and plastic foam insulation.

More recently, radiation concerns have joined chemical worries. Low-level radiation from electromagnetic fields (EMFs) emanating from

domestic electrical cabling and equipment, plus microwaves, have also been cited as potential problem areas. And radon (a naturally occurring radioactive gas in certain areas that can be carcinogenic at high levels) is now an officially recognized hazard. We are surrounded by a mass of electrical equipment, appliances and wiring in every room of the home. Added to this, there has been the sudden and massive growth in microwaves produced by mobile (cell) phones. Perhaps it is not surprising that controversy rages over whether or not our continual exposure to these low levels of radiation is another contributing factor to ill health and sick homes.

A house in harmony with its environment (above). This view was taken from the open-air eyrie – the eye of the hawk – high above SunHawk.

Simple things to keep your home healthy

- Never allow tobacco smoke inside the home.

- Use safe, nontoxic cleaners around the home.

- Keep the home clean and clutter-free.

- Open windows and skylights for periods to air the house.

- Avoid VOC-based paints and adhesives.

- Avoid formaldehyde-containing materials.

- Avoid synthetic textiles, carpets, and furnishings.

- Use an air ionizer.

- Fit "trickle vents" to windows.

- Install extractor fans in bathrooms and kitchens.

- Have gas-fired appliances checked and regularly maintained.

- Have your home checked for the presence of radon gas.

Sick building syndrome

Recurrent headaches, eye and nose irritation, dry throat, sleepiness, loss of concentration, and even nausea, can all be early-warning signs that your home may be "sick".

Although the term "sick building syndrome" was originally coined as a workplace malaise, occupants of modern homes can be challenged in similar ways. There is a disturbing increase in those suffering from allergies and "multiple chemical sensitivity" (MCS) – hypersensitivity to the modern chemical (and electronic) world. Your home may be only one contributing factor – office, factory, commuting, and even shopping in stores surrounded by synthetic materials can all impose a personal toxic overload. So it is wise to make sure that your home at least is as healthy and nontoxic as possible.

Ironically, part of this problem is an outcome of well-intentioned energy-conserving measures. For as we install draught-proofing, tighter-fitting windows and doors, plastic foam insulation, and block up old fireplace chimneys, our homes are in danger of becoming sealed boxes. Surrounded by impermeable materials, and with a less "leaky" construction, ventilation is dramatically reduced. Indoor pollutants then build up to harmful levels and are recirculated around the home.

Building for life

Exciting prospects for healthy building are offered by a fascinating concept called "baubiologie" (building biology). Originating in Germany, it combines a scientific and holistic view of the relationship of humans to their buildings. The house is likened to an organism and its walls to skin – a third skin (our clothes being the second). Like our skin, walls need to fulfil living functions: protecting, insulating, breathing, and regulating. And instead of trying to keep the outside separate from the inside, a healthful exchange is achieved via "breathing walls", which allow a gradual diffusion of air and moisture to regulate the indoor climate without loss of energy efficiency. Baubiologie prefers natural materials, as so many of them have in-built responsiveness. Hygroscopic (sponge-like) materials, such as clay, timber, lime plaster, and straw, for example,

when used properly, naturally absorb and release humidity and help modify indoor humidity and avoid condensation.

Traditional materials have been reintroduced and continual experimentation by baubiologie practitioners and institutes is improving older methods. As well as straw-bale building, timber frame breathing walls (see p. 44), other variants such as straw-clay (leichtlehm) are being employed successfully again (see p. 107). Radiant heating methods using traditional masonry stoves, tile ovens, or Finnish soapstone stoves once more grace living rooms with their elegant lines and nurturing warmth. You will know when you enter a home designed with baubiologie principles – it will feel clean and fresh, light and airy, and gently warm, with an aroma of natural materials and finishes – a healthy haven for relaxation and rejuvenation.

The living room in Tesuque Econest (above), inspired by baubiologie principles.

When the sun is in the right position, the projection of a hawk image coincides with the hawk motif on the floor of SunHawk (opposite).

Design for the spirit and harmony

Hand in hand with creating a healthy, sustainable building, you will want a home that is indeed *your* home. One that has meaning and individuality for you and your family; one that has a spirit of its own and brings happiness and good fortune; one that makes you feel secure and in harmony with yourself and the natural world. For ancient peoples of the world, the spiritual meaning of their homes and their surroundings were paramount. The home was often fashioned as a microcosm of their spirit world to ensure that it, and they, were intimately in harmony with their ancestors and their gods. Their communities, sacred buildings and surroundings were similarly laid out as "spiritual landscapes" to keep them in tune with the cosmos and seasonal cycles. Elaborate ceremonies would determine the *genius loci*, or sense of place, and small statues, stone tables, or earthen jars would be blessed and buried in the foundations to bring good luck and long life to the house and its occupants.

Today, although this has been lost in the Western world, there are still cultural memories and a yearning among many people to create a home that reconnects with these dimensions. The wave of popularity for feng shui – the ancient Chinese art of placement – has shown the extent of the desire for this. The traditional practice of dowsing has also enjoyed a revival. Houses are again designed to celebrate nature. Designs are even using the cardinal points and solar solstices and equinoxes (see p. 135).

Local historical contexts are another way to connect with your surroundings and acknowledge former inhabitants and traditions of the area (see pp. 28 and 92). Or, you may have personal affinities with traditional housing of other cultures, such as Japanese homes, or natural design movements, such as Arts and Crafts or organic architecture, and be inspired to embrace their qualities in your home (see p. 108).

There are many ways to find or create your spiritual home. Follow the path with the heart in it and you will be surprised where it will lead.

reduce your "footprint"

●

embody proximity

●

work with nature

●

make small changes

●

live off-grid

2 FUNK HOMESTEAD

The design of the homestead mirrors the organic qualities and unique spirit of the natural landscape, and acknowledges the history of the area – gold mining and, earlier, as a homeland of the Maidu Indians, who annually migrated from the Sacramento Valley below to the Sierra foothills of the site.

Michael Funk always dreamed of living in a wild place close to a river. "As a hiker, I knew and loved the Sierra foothills, and jumped at the chance to buy some land when it became available in this stunning area." And the land he purchased, with its steep, forested canyons, views of the Rock Creek waterfalls, and the rapids of the Yuba River gorge, became powerful and guiding inspirations when he and his family decided to build their home there. Working with local architect Jeff Gold, they carefully formulated their plans.

The house was not only to be a comfortable home for Michael and his family, it was also to be a place to share with guests. As well, it had to be suitable as a venue for gatherings of the local community groups they helped. The design was to be free and move "outside the box" to mirror the organic qualities and unique spirit of the natural landscape of the site.

A vision of the house began to emerge: an image of a sparkling natural gemstone with its many facets, each reflecting a special craft skill and an individual aspect of the rugged landscape. The final two-storey design revolved around a spacious central kiva-like living room with two curving wings. The westward wing reached out toward the river gorge and contained an open kitchen/dining area, while the eastward wing spread out toward the creek waterfalls and contained a home office/library and master bedroom and bathroom. A lower floor included guest bedrooms, entertainment areas, root cellar, and storage/maintenance areas.

The ancient Chinese art of placement, known as Feng Shui (meaning "wind and water"), was employed throughout the design process. It assisted with finding the most auspicious location on the site for the house, the location and layout of the internal spaces, and influenced the detailed design and construction decisions. Site characteristics, such as watershed, prevailing winds, sun movement, site contours, rock outcrops, tree cover, and wildlife habitat, were intimately studied and guided the design of the house so that it integrated harmoniously into the area.

The westward wing, looking out over the river gorge, expresses the house's link with nature (above).

" ... designing and building the Funk residence was a collective effort of hundreds of highly committed craftspeople, inspired by 'appropriate and caring action' – to create a locally rooted home that might last a hundred years or more ... One of the lasting memories of this project is the effort of setting stones with deliberation and without thought, so that each stone could, in a sense, be free to speak as we marvel at the beauty of the imperfect, seeming chaotic, natural world ..."

Jeff Gold, architect

The owners' personal commitment to the ecology movement and business involvement with organic foods meant their home had to be a place of health and healing. The project also had to be "sustainable". This resulted in the use of renewable energy sources, natural materials, nontoxic finishes, sensitivity to harvesting and manufacture of materials, and the use of local craftspeople. To lessen environmental impact and achieve the aim of a "sustainable building", the following practical features were to be incorporated:

A view of the south-facing kiva-like central living space (right) looking west toward the kitchen/dining area of the homestead.

Open space and natural habitat The creation of an organic garden and orchard, protected by deer-proof fencing, to produce year-round fruit and vegetables. The majority of the land to be retained as permanent open space and natural habitat. Walking trails to be established that were unobtrusive (frequently following the paths made by migrating deer).

Solar energy The property to be disconnected from the power grid and to rely on photovoltaic cells to produce electricity. Solar water heating panels to provide hot water and radiant underfloor heating. Emergency back-up electricity to be via a propane-gas-powered generator.

Water To be drawn from an on-site well and spring. Rainwater to be returned to the ground. Garden and orchard to be irrigated from the creek.

Passive solar heating Lower floor of the house to be built into the hillside to take advantage of even ground temperature. The upper floor to have extensive sun-facing windows, and interior floors and walls with heavy "thermal mass" to soak up and store the heat of the winter sun. Wide roof overhangs and shading devices, together with natural ventilation to prevent summer overheating and provide shade and comfort. Radiant floor heating to be fed by solar water panels.

Back-up heating A highly efficient Tulikivi woodburning soapstone stove to provide additional heat, if required, but expected to be needed only rarely. Deadwood and downwood to be the sole fuel used owing to its abundance on site.

Local materials and construction Local sources to be used wherever possible. Most of the stone for the exterior walls was gathered by hand on the site or collected from the local Sierra mountains. Stone was chosen for the exterior walls due to its local abundance, good thermal mass, and because of the potential danger of forest fires. All craftspeople and subcontractors came from the local community.

Recycled/salvaged hardwoods Recycled mahogany and jatoba for the doors and windows was sourced from a local supplier and a specialist wood-salvage company, which reclaims dead trees long-submerged under water.

Nontoxic materials Natural wood oils and wax plus water-based paints and finishes, inert fillers and non-formaldehyde-containing materials used. Spray-applied cotton insulation (from recycled blue jeans) for walls and ceilings. Wool rugs with jute backing over felt for guest bedrooms.

Wood The use of native wood species connects the Funk homestead to its forest setting. The dominant woods used are two indigenous species: Douglas fir for the framing and western red cedar for exterior boarding and trim FSC-certified (Forest Stewardship Council) from a local mill.

Master building process

During the two-year construction period, architect Jeff Gold also acted as builder and took the opportunity to practise the traditional art of "master building". This meant he could infuse the building process with a creative spirit and collaborate more closely with people and materials. An on-going "conversation" enabled the original design to be refined as the building took shape. Subcontractors were encouraged to make suggestions to improve the original design. Sometimes, parts of the house were laid out full scale on the ground without the aid of drawings. Both major changes and minor adjustments were made daily – for example, the placement of the large boulders that connect the structure to the natural landscape. As the building took shape, the owners participated in every stage and appreciated being able to review the designs and make their preferences for the detailed finishes known. This "organic" process allowed the house to grow, not only from the original design, but also more directly out of the building process – materials, techniques, craftspeople, and owners all contributing to making the Funk Homestead a truly beautiful and sustainable home.

The master bedroom with terrace and window seating (above) looking out toward the creek waterfalls.

eco data

CONSTRUCTION
- Stone walls from locally gathered granite rocks and boulders
- Local craftspeople used as contractors

MATERIALS
- Recycled and salvaged timber used as much as possible
- Reclaimed submerged, old-growth timber
- FSC-certified sourcing of Douglas fir and western red cedar
- Nontoxic, non-formaldehyde-containing materials and finishes
- Recycled cotton insulation
- Wool carpets with jute backing over felt underlay
- Natural oil and wax finishes

ENERGY SYSTEM
- Off-grid, 35kW photovoltaic panel system with 82 (Astro Power 120w modules) plus inverters and battery storage
- Back-up propane-gas-powered generator (GENSAT system)

HEATING
- Passive solar and storage via heavy thermal mass
- Radiant floor heating by solar water panels
- Back-up heating by Tulikivi soapstone wood-burning stove using downwood from property

COOLING
- Natural cross-ventilation and convection
- Shading by wide roof overhangs and window devices
- Earth-linked lower floor and cellar help to moderate temperature

WATER
- On-site well
- On-site spring irrigates landscape and organic garden
- Rainwater harvested and returned to creek
- Water heating via solar water panels
- Greywater-separation system

LANDSCAPE
- Organic garden and orchard, large wilderness and wildlife areas

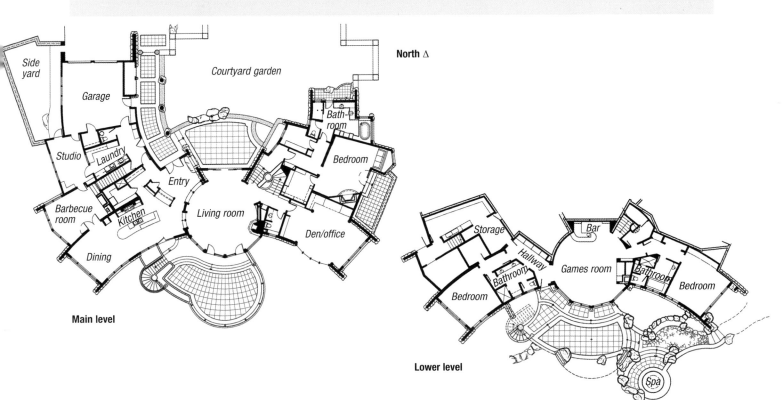

North △

Main level

Lower level

CHAPTER 2

choosing your approach

An individual home in the country (above) or an urban cohousing scheme plus a communal house (opposite) – these are just two of the different approaches to creating a natural home.

You now know the basic principles for making your home a natural home. Next, you need to consider what is possible and achievable in your individual circumstances. Take stock of your lifestyle and plan how you want to "green" it, and when. What power do you have to make these changes? Are you renting? Are you buying your first home? Have you thought of joining or forming an eco-community and living there? Whatever your age, income, health, or experience, and wherever you happen to live – city, suburb, or country – you *can* make your home green and healthy. What will differ, depending on your circumstances, will be your priorities, time, budget, and involvement.

The beginning
This is the starting-out stage when you are full of enthusiasm, but short on experience. Money may be tight, but, if you are reasonably healthy and energetic, you can cut costs substantially by doing a lot of the work yourself. If you are living in a rental unit, you will probably be restricted as to what you can change by the lease or agreement. However, landlords often encourage improvements and some offer an initial rent-free period as an inducement if you do the work.

If you are an owner-occupier, you will have more freedom and incentive. Depending on your budget and preferences, affordable projects to consider include decorating using eco-paints and recycled/reclaimed materials, "greening" your kitchen (see pp. 146–7) and bathroom (see pp. 148–9), and installing soft-energy systems and water-saving equipment (see pp. 152–5).

Rather than going it alone and "greening" your individual apartment or house, it is worth investigating communal options. You may, for example, be able to buy into a "green" housing project, such as Green Condo (see pp. 76–81), or Springfield Cohousing (see pp. 40–5). Or, you could choose to join a self-build community, such as Earthship (see pp. 64–9), or an eco-village (see pp. 152–5) and build your own house with the help and support of the community. However, these projects are much in demand and there are relatively few of them about, so put your name down early and expect a long wait.

Alternatively, you could join with others who want a new home and form a cooperative housing group. Unless the group is well advanced or a member drops out, then the time from start-up to moving in to your new home could take years, but it is usually well worth the wait.

Low-budget tips for beginners

• Fit draught-proofing to doors and windows.

• Hang thermal linings behind curtains (drapes) or make thermally insulated indoor window shutters.

• Visit recycling dumps and house clearances and look for free or low-cost solid wood furniture and shelving, light fittings, door handles, and so on.

• Visit jumble sales, yard sales, flea-markets, and charity (thrift) stores and look for wool, cotton, or linen textiles, curtains (drapes), wall hangings, wool rugs, cushions, and light fittings.

• Redecorate walls and paint used furniture with nontoxic paints and stains and strippers. Take care when stripping old paint as it may contain lead.

• Use natural, nontoxic household cleaners.

• Recycle all paper, card, cans, plastic, and glass bottles.

• Compost all organic kitchen waste.

• Grow fresh herbs and salad in window boxes.

Moving on

So, a few years have gone by and you have cut your teeth on your first projects. Circumstances are changing, you have a new relationship or the family is growing up, and it is time to upgrade your present home or move on to another. You may be earning more and are able to consider more ambitious eco-projects. Whether you are staying or moving on, this is the time to invest as much as you can afford in the future.

Upgrades for your new house might include installing or enlarging the photovoltaic system with more modules and storage, or installing or enlarging the capacity of the solar water heating system, and perhaps adding radiant underfloor heating. Other options could range from adding rainwater catchment and greywater recycling to setting up a permaculture garden.

When deciding, think ahead to your next lifecycle stage. If you plan to retire, it is wise to

invest in items that will save running costs later, when finances may be more constrained. Even if you move away later, these investments are sure to increase your home's value.

With these more expensive projects, you need to calculate their pay-back period – the time it takes the estimated savings in running costs to repay the capital outlay – to see if they make sense economically. It is also a good idea to check if you are eligible for any government grants or loans (for solar energy, for example). And take advice from well-established local

Upgrade and new project ideas

• Upgrade wall and roof insulation.

• Upgrade your kitchen appliances to highest-efficiency, low-energy models.

• Green your kitchen with non-formaldehyde-containing units and reclaimed materials for counter tops and floor finishes.

• Green your bathroom with a low-volume flush toilet and low-flow shower.

• Install a greywater recycling system and fit a heat-exchanger to recoup "greywater" heat.

• Upgrade and enlarge the capacity of your photovoltaic and/or your solar hot-water system.

• Install a solar conservatory (sunspace) with thermal mass storage and internal planting.

• Remodel your yard or garden to be a permaculture plot, plus wildlife pond, and grow organic vegetables, herbs, and salads.

• Install or upgrade rainwater harvesting, and your greywater (and blackwater, if possible) cleansing and reuse systems.

estate agents (realtors) on how they might best add sale value to your property.

Dan and Debbie helped to self-build Tree House for their family as a pilot project for a proposed larger development (see pp. 52–7). Robert and Paula have gained a wealth of experience from building and living in a series of "econest" healthy houses (see pp. 104–9). Annie and Patsy moved into Orchard House (see pp. 120–5) after helping the architect with some of the work themselves, such as building the sculptural cob fireplace.

Creating the Econest healthy houses (above left) was a continuing learning experience for Robert and Paula, with each new home teaching them something new about the next.

Arriving

It is said that to travel hopefully is a better thing than to arrive. And it is true that most of the fun and meaning in life is in doing things rather than sitting back and observing. It is in this spirit that you come to the time when, if you are determined and fortunate, you will achieve your dreams and live in your ideal natural home. But dreams, like mirages, can be strangely fickle. As you draw near, they can fade away and you have to find another dream.

It is like this with a natural home. It is never really finished, it is always emerging and in a state of flux. It is a sort of life-long experiment in which some things you try work beautifully, while others are a dismal failure. After all, many ecological building techniques and systems are still relatively new, and it takes a while to see how they stand the test of time. So, although you may come to live in your dream natural home and enjoy it as you surely should, expect it to change and be just a stage on the way. The important thing is to take delight in every step.

Michael had already built four houses before Spiral House (see pp. 90–5) yet, having done all this, he had a distinct twinkle in his eye when he spoke of his plans for a cooperative community organic farm. The Funk Homestead (see pp. 28–33) came into being through an on-going "conversation" between architect, client, and craftspeople – all part of the "master building" process. Some elements of the design were predetermined, but some were allowed to evolve during the building. And, as with all houses, some more will continue to evolve over time.

John and Nancy have invested decades of solar design experience in SunHawk (see pp. 134–9), which incorporates some of the latest technology and recycled-content materials. And although these may change and be upgraded in time, the timeless circular design of the house will always be in harmony with the diurnal cycle of the sun and nocturnal path of the moon. Perhaps Henry Yorke Mann, architect of Posts Standing (see pp. 14–19) puts it best in his poem on the right.

Timeless settings for dream natural homes – SunHawk (opposite top) and the Funk Homestead (opposite below).

Flowing

Combining

Separating

Reforming

Mutating

Coalescing

in

the

God

Dance

3 SPRINGFIELD COHOUSING

Community housing grouped around a pedestrian "street", this lively "village" is roofed with solar tiles and landscaped with water management in mind. Individual houses and apartments are purchased by prospective residents, who are able to influence the design of their homes and also have access to communal facilities.

Stroud, often referred to as "the greenest town in the west", has the largest LETS (Local Exchange Trading System) alternative currency scheme in the UK. The town also has a green mayor heading a green town council, and is host to many initiatives, including a thriving farmers' market, organic and wholefood cafés, natural health practices, and a growing network of talented artists and musicians. So when property developer David Michael found that a large site on the edge of town was up for sale, he and his wife, Helen, put in a successful bid. "As soon as I'd done it, I thought I must be mad to take on all this responsibility", says David. But when in a few weeks enough people had come forward to buy plots, he realized "it might just work after all!"

In fact, 30 per cent of the plots were presold before legal completion of the land purchase. And it is not surprising when you see the south-facing sloping site. Only a few minutes' walk from town and bordered with mature trees, it enjoys views across the beautiful Slad Valley.

Before forming The Cohousing Company Ltd, David appointed architects Jono Hines of Architype and Pat Borer of the Centre of Alternative Technology to help create the green community design. Inspired by the two seminal books on the subject – *Cohousing* by Kathryn McCarrant and Charles Durrett, and *A Pattern Language* by Christopher Alexander et al – and informed by their wide knowledge of ecohousing, the designers came up with a scheme for 35 houses and flats, ranging from studios to 4- or 5-bedroomed units, grouped around the hub of a communal house.

Central to the design is the pedestrianized layout. Car parking is kept to the periphery and pedestrian walkways link the houses and make for a safe, quiet environment. A Sustainable Urban Drainage System (SUDS) deals with site rainwater, which is conducted through a series of swales, ponds, and rills (soon to be planted with aquatic plants) that run beside the walkways. Excess water that has not soaked into the ground, flows into a nearby stream, and in very

What is cohousing?

Put simply, it is a cooperative process whereby people create their own housing. There may be many different routes to this final goal – as in this example, the process can begin with a developer who finds the land, appoints an architect, and brings people together to invest. Or, it can be a group who initiate and manage the whole process. The concept combines privacy with community. Each household has its own self-contained accommodation, yet meets and shares facilities in a large communal house. Originally started in Denmark in the 1970s, cohousing is now gaining in popularity around the world, and especially in the USA, where there are now more than 30 cohousing communities.

The generous outdoor balcony space (opposite) has views across to the Cotswold hills.

On this steeply sloping hillside site, the houses step down and are linked by walkways (above). The banks are supported by "gabions" – cages filled with stones.

A retaining wall (left) showing the red terracotta pipes of the SUDS water system.

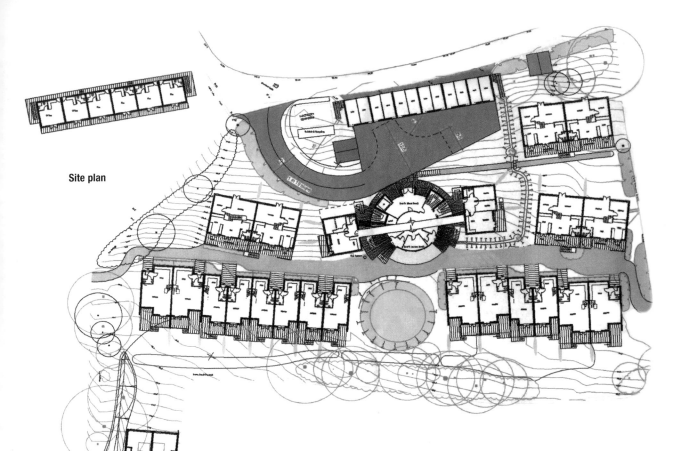

Site plan

A sun-facing, open-plan space (opposite) doing duty as a living room, kitchen, and dining area. The door leads out onto a terrace.

heavy rainfall temporarily fills a grassy soakaway (drywell) area that doubles as a "village" green.

The timber-framed houses are all designed to a high standard of energy-efficiency and are specified with green materials wherever possible. Large areas of photovoltaic roof tiles on every house produce communal electricity – making it the largest residential system so far in the UK – with any excess electricity produced being sold to the grid.

With an interest in environmental issues and sustainable living, historic building surveyor (and now local Green Party councillor) Sarah Lunnon was looking for somewhere congenial to relocate when she happened to see the Stroud project mentioned in a newspaper article on cohousing. But when she made contact via the project web-site (see p. 152), all the plots had been sold. However, when an early member had to resell a plot, Sarah was in luck.

Coming to the project just before her house was built, Sarah and her partner, performance

artist James Lee, have been actively involved in the final stages of the development. They admit it has not all been plain sailing. First, they had some difficulty in raising a mortgage on their new house, owing to the project's unfamiliarity and the houses being built of timber, which is unusual in the UK. But they did find a sympathetic bank and all was well.

Then (despite advice to the contrary from cohousing books), there was a consensus among scheme members that they could customize the interior of their units to meet individual preferences. This resulted in almost every house plan being slightly different regarding the positions of internal, non-load-bearing walls, kitchen locations, kitchen and bathroom fixtures, and even bedroom adaptations to provide extra storage areas. And, along with all this, came the variations in electric and plumbing systems.

Although this gave each household a lot of flexibility, it did result in a mass of extra work for the architects and builder, and an inevitable

CONSTRUCTION
- Timber-frame clad with cement render on Heraklith wood-wool board and UK-grown Douglas fir cladding
- Timber-boarded roofs covered with Redland concrete tiles and BP photovoltaic tiles

MATERIALS
- Sustainably harvested Douglas fir from Shropshire
- Nontoxic materials, organic paints, and stains
- Blown-in cellulose insulation from recycled newspaper by "Warmcell"

SOFT ENERGY SYSTEM
- Total 49kW communal photovoltaic system: large houses 3kW; medium houses 2.5kW; small houses 2kW via BP modules supplied by Sundog
- Grid EDF energy buys back excess electricity
- Plus inverters and meters in each house

HEATING
- Passive solar via south-facing windows
- High-performance windows and doors triple-glazed from Sweden Window Company
- Water-filled radiators heated by conventional gas-fired boilers, all ready for retro-fitting of solar thermal roof panels

COOLING
- High insulation levels reduce need
- Natural ventilation via windows and balcony doors
- Open roof slopes and high-level Velux rooflights give passive ventilation/cooling
- Roof overhangs to shade summer sun

WATER
- SUDS (Sustainable Urban Drainage System) – rainwater rills running via soakaway (drywell) to local stream reduces site run-off
- Water-conserving IFO low-flush toilets
- Water heating by individual gas-fired boilers. Solar water panels to follow

LANDSCAPE
- Communal areas to be planted with native species
- Small pond to encourage wildlife
- Communal vegetable garden, compost, and free-range chickens
- Food cooperative planned

An internal stairwell, looking downward from the upper landing (opposite, top).

"Paddle stairs" leading up to the children's mezzanine play area (opposite, below).

The communal house (left) consists of three floors: the first level is for "dirty" work, workshops, and so on; the second level is used as a communal kitchen/dining area; and the third level is a "clean" space used for choir meetings and similar activities.

The old yew tree (below), where the children's tree-house is planned to be built.

addition to the project's budget. Therefore, economies had to be made along the way and some of the original features, such as rainwater recycling, lime render, and the communal house turf roof, were reluctantly sacrificed. In addition, some members accepted hand-over of their homes in a less-than-complete state internally. This allowed them to spread the costs and introduce their own finishes, such as internal decoration, tiling, floor finishes, and light fixtures. Some even elected to buy and fit their own internal doors. "There was too much choice really," say Sarah and James, "and some compromises had to be made." If they were involved in another project they would definitely want a project manager to help keep the work on track and on budget.

Many of the more intimate communal features (inspired by the book *A Pattern Language*) such

"The radical design of both site layout and houses reflects the very different agenda of cohousing as compared with any other housing in the UK. We are delighted to have played our part in helping to shape this innovative and forward-looking community."
Jono Hines, architect

as the outdoor decks and front porches overlooking the main pedestrian street have fostered informal contact between the residents. "It was lovely last summer," recalls Sarah, "to sit out on the cool of the front porch and say 'Hello' to everyone as they passed by."

The opening of the communal house will be a real boost, with communal meals, woodworking and textile workshop facilities, laundry, and a large, open room ideal for parties, celebrations, and regular member meetings. "We already have a small choir and a gardening group," continues Sarah, "and there's lots of ideas coming from the new people moving in." James points out of the window to a pile of salvaged timber under a large yew tree, "When the builders have gone, we're going to build a treehouse for all the children in the community."

CHAPTER 3

getting started

A dream site for SunHawk (opposite). The design was inspired by the roundhouse of the local Native Americans and it has a magnificent terrace view of Duncan Peak.

Renovating or extending an existing property may sound simpler than building new, but there can be pitfalls resulting in extra time, stress, and cost. Older buildings often have hidden problems that come to light only when the builder starts work. These may be structural – a wall thought to be load-bearing found to be only a partition, or a lintel thought to be steel found to be only timber. Or they may be due to condition – penetrating damp found to have caused more extensive wood rot than first expected.

Before you make plans and budgets, it is best to have your property surveyed by a qualified professional. A full survey should itemize and give cost estimates for all areas requiring remedial work. To do this the surveyor may need to "open up" some test areas to see what is underneath. Any repair items can then be built into your over-all renovation plans. But, to be on the safe side, include extra funds in your budget (and builder's priced specification) for "unforeseen works".

Before deciding on extending a house, check with the local planning office to find out what is permitted. If the extension is below a certain size or type, it may be allowed without permission as a "permitted development". Conservatories and some small garden buildings, for instance, may

be exempted if they meet certain criteria. But generally, if you want to extend the house upward or outward you will need permission. And if the house is within a conservation area or is a listed building of special architectural interest, then there are more controls on what you can do. Specialist companies, such as those doing loft conversions or installing conservatories, will usually handle all the permissions for you.

For new-build, unless you opt for a predesigned package where the supplier deals with the whole process, from permissions to construction, you will need to consider your role. Although you can undertake the whole process yourself, it is best, if not essential, to use the services of an architect (see p. 50) to help, at least, formulate ideas and produce drawings to gain planning approval. Beyond this, you may want to "self-build" all or part of your home (see pp. 51 and 70) or use a builder to complete the whole job.

Whatever decided on – renovating or extending an existing property or going for new-build – you will be faced with similar questions. Do I need an architect? Can I do self-build? Are there kits or packages I can use? How do I find a good builder and specialist craftspeople? And, in the case of new-build, how do I find a suitable site?

Finding a site

Choosing a good plot for your natural home may be more challenging than you expect. Think ecologically and remember that the best traditional habitats grow out of the place, and reflect its spirit, microclimate, soil, vegetation, and wildlife. But before looking for a site, you need some basic ideas of the sort of home you want – approximate size, facilities, orientation, and outside space. In addition, if the house is in close proximity to schools, work, and leisure amenities, it will not only be more convenient, but it will also save on car transport, pollution, and energy.

You might at this stage consider proceeding individually to find a single plot or investigate joining a group enterprise, such as cohousing or sustainable community. The advantage of a joint venture is that a site may have already been found where you can buy a plot. More than this, you may benefit from being part of a supportive and like-minded group and share their ecobuilding expertise. For example, Sarah and James (see pp. 40–5) found their plot in the Springfield Cohousing project, while the Earthship sustainable community offers sites and building packages (see pp. 64–9). Or, you can opt for up-and-coming eco-development projects, such as Green Condo (see pp. 76–81), where you can put your name down for a new, stylish eco-apartment.

Sometimes an awkward or seemingly imperfect site can be transformed. It is likely to be more affordable and, in the case of Robert and Paula (see pp. 104–9), they created the now-beautiful site for their Econest community by dint of hard work and imaginative landscaping. Changes in the agriculture market can also produce possible sites, as it did fortuitously for Patsy and Annie (see pp. 120–5), when a mature apple orchard fell into disuse and was sold off as a plot.

But if you have luck on your side and the resources, there are some truly magnificent sites to be found. Michael (see pp. 28–33) found his dream river gorge site because he knew the area intimately and had walked it for years. John and Nancy (see pp. 134–9) located a stunning hilltop site close to their business, Real Goods, so their home could be shared for courses on solar living and permaculture. Bruce and Lynno (see pp. 14–19) wanted a quiet retreat from their hectic business lives, and so settled for a secluded waterfront island lot. In all of these, the challenge was to preserve the beauty of the site, and to design and place the home within the site in order to minimize environmental impact.

Allow plenty of time to search for potential sites. Once you have narrowed down the area where you want to relocate, try local estate agents (realtors), local newspapers, property magazines, local councils, and utility companies (who may be selling off sites); ask friends, family, and work colleagues to keep a lookout, and even place an advert. Property websites and auctions are other possible sources. But for eco and healthy homes, also contact specialist organizations and groups (see pp. 152–5) who may know of new housing projects you could join. Just keep talking to as many contacts as possible and something is likely to turn up – in time.

The sloping foothill site of Tree House, shown in the spring (opposite).

El Valle, the verdant view the Kaufmanns could not resist when building their natural home, Spiral House (below). The house itself is just to the right of this picture.

Whether you are moving to an existing property or planning to build your own home, look for a balance of the following when choosing a site:

• Good solar aspect. A site with unrestricted sun where you need it, especially in winter. This allows the year-round efficient use of passive solar design and active solar energy equipment.

• Protection from prevailing winds and summer heat by landform and/or mature trees and shrubs. Investigate local wind currents or strong seasonal winds for best house location on site.

• Away from flooding and landslides. Avoid low-lying sites on floodplains or where there is a history of landslides. Remember that flooding is on the increase in some areas.

• Good, well-drained soil. The right soil assists with organic gardening, permaculture and growing your own food.

• Natural water supply. Natural springs and wells are a bonus if you can find a site with them. A stream or creek may be useful for hydropower.

• Avoid natural and man-made hazards. Check site radon levels and underground "geopathic" zones (watercourses, electromagnetic radiation). Avoid microwave masts, proximity to high-voltage power lines, and other sources of pollution.

• A sense of place. A site with good spirit (feng shui) that inspires your individual sense of belonging. A site that will make you say "this is my place".

Do you need an architect?

"First find yourself a good architect," advises experienced timber-framer and eco-builder Robert Laporte whenever he is asked how to build a natural home. And his partnership with talented architect Paula Baker has certainly proved the point (see pp. 104–9). Although many people feel they can go it alone, it is wise to consult a professional at the earliest stage if you are contemplating extending your home or building a new one. Architects are trained to solve problems creatively and coordinate all stages of the design and building process. They can save time and money and, if right for you and your project, can ensure that you end up with a natural home that is sustainable, healthy, and stylish.

An example of when many hands do make light of the work – here (opposite), erecting a timber frame.

Finding the right architect

It is as important to find the right architect as it is to find the right site. Research is vital – more so, as you are planning a natural house, which requires architectural knowledge, experience, and sympathy with ecological design, healthy building, and the less-definable and personal area of "spirit".

The good news is that there is a growing number of architects with a good track record in these areas. Look through magazines, particularly the specialist ones, search online, and contact local architects' institutes, and eco-architects' and builders' associations (see pp. 152–5).

Before making a choice, draw up a shortlist of likely architects and then contact them to see if they are available. If so, request literature, outlines of each firm's experience, and a portfolio of relevant work. Discuss services and fees and ask to visit finished projects you like and, above all, talk to the architect to see if you are compatible.

A good working relationship between you and your architect is crucial to success. And before any design work starts, ensure you have a written agreement appointing your architect and containing details of the agreed scope of services and fees. Professional institutes publish standard agreements, including one for "small works", falling below a certain cost.

design work. But if you decide to go the self-build route, then you will probably be dealing directly with the main contractor/builder without the help of an architect.

Finding the right contractor/builder is a similar process to finding the right architect – ask for personal recommendations, make a shortlist, obtain quotes, visit recent work, conduct interviews and discussions, check qualifications and experience, and inspect insurance policies. Then, once you have selected your builder, make sure you have a good contract (checked over by your legal adviser) with contract drawings and building specifications appended. Standard building contracts are available from the relevant professional bodies.

But there are many variations. For example, you may want to act as the main contractor yourself. If so, you will need to hire and project manage the building team and subcontractors yourself. And if you have the skills, you may also want to help with hands-on work on site, as did Michael Kauffman when he helped build the Spiral House (see pp. 90–5).

There is a range of other options that blurs the conventional distinctions between architect and builder. One of these is "master building". Jeff Gold doubled as architect and builder for the Funk Homestead (see pp. 28–33) and directed what he called "an on-going conversation" between the design and building aspects of the project as it proceeded. This enhanced dialogue and collaboration between the hundreds of craftspeople involved led to an extremely successful result. A similar happy experience occurred when architect Darrel DeBoer worked with builder Tim Owen-Kennedy (see p. 121). Traditional boundaries fell away as both men developed the plans – Tim producing architectural details and Darrel working on site.

"Partnership" is the watchword for a good building team. In all the featured examples in this book the relationships between client, architect, builder, and craftspeople became a special journey of discovery.

Finding a builder

How you find and relate to a builder depends on the role you want to adopt. If, for example, you are using the full services of an architect, then these will include recommending a shortlist of main contractors to tender for the contract. However, it is still worth you interviewing the suggested builders, seeing some of the work they have produced, and asking the owners how they responded to the process. It is not always the best policy to accept the lowest tender price. Other factors – such as crafts skills, sympathy, and experience with eco and healthy materials, and the ability to source recycled and reclaimed items – will all count, too.

Alternatively, if you use a design-build company, you will be hiring a builder working in combination with an architect to produce the

4 TREE HOUSE

The design explores the idea of contact with earth and sky. This is expressed by carving one end of the house into the hillside and rooting it well into the earth, while the other end is extended upward toward the sky, like a bird's wing – almost as if it wants to fly.

Although Dan and Debbie Priest had no previous experience in building a house, Dan did have woodworking knowledge and wanted to create a home that expressed the fine qualities of that material. He also wanted to be able to see the wood structure of the house designed and built with what he termed "exposed structural craftsmanship".

The couple were committed to living an environmentally friendly lifestyle and were, therefore, determined to build a house that was not only healthy and "green", but also one that would set an example for the best in modern domestic architectural design.

Having acquired a large tract of land at 900m (3,000ft) elevation in the foothills of the Sierra Nevada Mountains, Dan went further than just thinking about his own family's home. He saw the potential for something more ambitious. As an area of outstanding beauty, he wanted to demonstrate how housing could be designed to be more compact and less wasteful of land than current local standards.

The site was ideal for a small community of families with children, especially with the adjacent local elementary school and the easy access of the site to the local village of Camino. So he envisioned a plan to create a discrete number of houses clustered on the site in "islands" to limit disruption to the landscape, maintain natural drainage, and allow for wildlife migration through the site. Separate communal buildings would be added to provide additional amenities, such as guest accommodation and recreation facilities.

To start the process rolling, the owners commissioned Paul Almond and Pam Whitehead of Sage Architecture to come up with a prototype house for them to live in with their two children, one that would serve to highlight the main features that the houses in the larger community would ultimately have.

A primary goal of the development was to limit the size of houses and their impact on the land. So, with this in mind, a relatively small structure called Tree House was devised to be the first test case. This was actually conceived

Seen here (above) in spring and set among verdant, wooded slopes, the house truly expresses its name – Tree House. Open to the sun and air, yet sheltered by the hill, the floor-to-ceiling windows look out over the valley below.

as being a "slice" taken out of what would be one of the main house designs – a sectional cut that embodies its features.

Set in a small, natural clearing among deciduous and evergreen trees, the house is on a south-facing slope with distant mountain views. Several large, mature oak trees grow on the site and the location of the house was chosen sensitively so that none of these was disturbed and that, indeed, one of them even helped to give shade to the house.

With a clear goal that the residence should respond directly to its environment, physically and conceptually, the idea was to produce a design that would heat and cool the house using a combination of natural ventilation and passive solar features. Debbie had a dislike for forced-air heating as well as artificial air conditioning, so natural methods had to be used. Basic laws of thermodynamics were used to sculpt the form of the building – a simple shed-like form with a mono-pitch roof was the simple solution. With windows placed at the highest point on the south and west elevations, and others sited at low level on opposite sides, cool air could be drawn in at ground level and hot air expelled from the top. To regulate indoor temperatures further, the lower part at the rear of the structure is built into the hillside, and the roof construction is vented above and below its plywood decking.

Another feature is a two-storey wooden lattice built against the west-side exterior staircase to shade the house from afternoon summer sun. With the extra insulation Dan installed, the wood stove that provides winter heating and radiant underfloor heat to the ground slab is hardly ever used. Although the house has proved comfortable, Paul Almond admits that if they build further houses here, they will orient them about 10° more to the east to reduce exposure to summer sun from south and west.

Viewed looking up from the hill slope, the house appears lightweight and airy among the trees and is rightly named Tree House. Private areas, such as the bedrooms, are positioned to

Looking into the deck-level family room from the south-facing terrace (above), the doors slide back to create an open, alfresco living space.

The living areas are split (right) – the lower level looks toward the kitchen, the upper level looks toward the bedrooms.

the rear in the carved-out portion to express enclosure and protection. A transitional zone in the middle contains kitchen/dining areas, closets, and bathrooms. Public areas, such as the living and play rooms, are located where the building opens outward and upward, culminating in two large sliding glass panels that meet at the dematerialized southeast corner. These, in turn, slide open to lead out onto the raised deck, and the sky.

Dan and Debbie have both helped with the construction of the house. The family lived in a trailer on the site while the house was being built, and say they loved living the outdoor life. Dan acted as builder up to the first floor before the winter set in, and then used another builder to complete the second floor and roof. He then finished the house in the spring – the whole process having taken about a year. But there are still things than need to be done. One of these is adding solar electricity, as planned for in the design, when funds permit.

Even though Tree House has earned a series of prestigious awards from the American Institute of Architects, at present Dan has not managed to persuade the local town council to give its permission to develop the land any further toward his ultimate goal. But he will continue to try and, in the meantime, Debbie continues to teach yoga, dance, and martial arts and is in the process of creating a permaculture garden, complete with rainwater pond. Dan continues to work as a builder elsewhere and lives in hope that one day he will make his dream of a sustainable community a reality.

A dramatically angled view showing the wood-burning stove and stove pipe used for back-up heating in very cold weather (above left).

The upper living area (left) has fine views over the forested valley below.

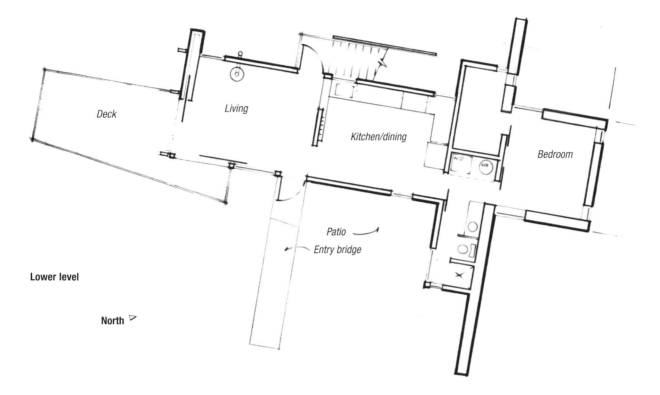

Deck

Living

Kitchen/dining

Bedroom

Patio

Entry bridge

Lower level

North ▷

eco data

CONSTRUCTION
• Locally sourced timber
• Some recycled, salvaged and/or reclaimed materials

MATERIALS
• Salvaged redwood boarding
• Nontoxic materials and finishes
• Non-VOC paints
• Water-based stains

ENERGY SYSTEM
• Photovoltaic system to be installed later

HEATING
• Passive solar heat via large, south-facing windows
• Radiant floor heating powered by propane gas water heater (rarely needed). Solar water heating planned
• Back-up wood-burning stove

COOLING
• Large tree shades building
• Vented roof space
• Orientation and positioning of windows
• Window-shading devices
• Natural ventilation and "stack effect"
• Lower floor buried in ground helps to moderate temperature

WATER
• Rainwater harvesting for irrigation
• Water heated via propane gas heater
• Solar water heating planned

LANDSCAPE
• Small footprint of building
• Permaculture garden and pond
• Wildlife protection
• Plans for sustainable community

creating your design

Themes and variations from nature: the spiral form of a nautilus shell (above) that inspired the Kauffmans in the design of their very individual natural home.

Cappadocia, Turkey (opposite), where the soft tufa stone is ideal for creating cave homes that blend into the landscape.

Creating designs for your natural home is one of the most exciting and fulfilling stages of the process. This is when you, and your family, are free to express your dreams before they have to be tempered by the realities of regulations, schedules, and cost. Before going to an architect or designer (if you plan to use one), allow plenty of time to formulate your own ideas. But bear in mind that, as well as conventional requirements, the overall design for your natural home will need to combine and balance the three main elements of sustainability, healthy building, and spirit (see p. 20).

Some ideas spring from a personal theme or image that becomes a powerful force in the design – a spiral form for Michael and Mahabba (see p. 90), a multi-faceted gemstone for Michael Funk (see p. 28), or a child's tree house for Dan and Debbie (see p. 52).

Others arise out of materials and locality. Camp out in your new site and let it "speak" to you. Observe how the sun and wind move, how the wildlife lives, and how your feelings respond, just as John and Nancy (see p. 136) did to settle on the ideal place for their house. And on the subject of materials, there are fashions with these just as there are with clothes. So resist the temptation to jump at straw bale or cob, for example, which, although perfectly good materials, may not be suitable for your design or site.

Inspirations come from many quarters and the main thing is to let them come. Of course, books, magazines, and television are the usual sources for would-be home designers. Bruce and Lynno (see p. 14) made a scrapbook of pictures of homes they admired to show their architect. These sources are very useful, but first reach into your own imagination. Think carefully of your living patterns – would open plan suit you or are you more comfortable with separate rooms?

As well as writing down your ideas, make some rough concept sketches. These do not have to be works of art – some scribbles will do! They will help you visualize your ideas and begin to see them in three-dimensional form. However, it has to be said that conflicts can arise when couples and family members participate. Your ideas may be quite different from those of your partner, let alone those of younger members of the household. Very stressful situations occur when each begins to dig in his or her heels. Usually discussion and compromise solve the problem and the early assistance of an architect or a designer can help avoid this.

Design process

Having formulated your ideas and concepts, the next stage is to confront reality and turn these into plans, specifications, and costs – and obtain the necessary approvals. If you are going to use a professional, such as an architect, that person should be properly appointed (see p. 50). Meet with your architect and discuss your project in more detail, the scope of works envisaged, and the services needed. Your architect will guide you through this and explain what is most appropriate to your circumstances. Architects usually divide the work into a series of stages that are incorporated in the professional standard form of client/architect agreement.

The basic services are: outline proposals (scheme design), detailed design (design development), production information (construction documents), and building tenders (bids), followed by supervision of the construction works on site. A host of other non-basic services is also offered, including predesign feasibility studies, planning appeals, property condition reports, structural surveys, landscape design, environmental analysis, and more. For some of these, the use of a specialist consultant will be advised or, alternatively, you can specify one you wish to employ. Fees for basic services can be based on a percentage of the total construction cost, on time expended, or on a lump sum. They are paid either as each stage is completed or monthly on invoice.

You can opt to use all of the basic services or some of them. For example, the architect could be asked to provide only plans, specifications, and obtain all approvals, leaving you to cope with the rest of the project. This may save on architect's fees, but it leaves you to deal with the builder and supervise work on site. Unless you are very experienced, or very lucky, this may end up being time consuming, stressful, and expensive. There is a saying: "even the simplest of projects are very complex". Designing and building a house is certainly not simple, so it is probably better if you are going to use an architect at all, to use him or her to do the whole job from start to finish.

Research

A lot of fun can be had researching other houses and the marketplace for "green" materials and products. The best time to do this is early on, while you are coming up with concept design ideas for your new home, so your discoveries can be fed into the process. As well as searching in books, magazines, and surfing the web, visit local green stores and green building material suppliers, and arrange visits to other local natural homes and eco-showhouses, or join green or solar-home open-day tours. You can even rent a show home, such as an Earthship, for the weekend.

Summer is a good time to go to eco-festivals, which are now so popular they are held annually in many towns and cities. These are great places to network and make new contacts. The green world can be a small place and often you find that everyone knows everyone else in the locality.

Taking things further, you can join an environmental design or building association (see pp. 152–5). These offer a wealth of information, experience, and contacts, and you should attend local meetings and annual gatherings or conferences. For a more hands-on approach, sign up for building courses and workshops to learn how to be a timber-framer or build with straw bale, adobe, bamboo, and other green materials. Visit local reclamation or architectural salvage companies to select used items to incorporate into your overall design. Visit craft fairs and workshops to find craftspeople you like.

Design concepts: the flowing organic forms of Gaudi (top); the woven spiral roof of a traditional Shona hut from Zimbabwe (above); and architect Renzo Piano's first sketch for the Kanak Cultural Centre (left).

Budget, costs, and funding

While you are dreaming about your beautiful new home, it is salutary and tempering to begin thinking about the budget and what you can actually afford. You can get a rough idea of what this might be by using the "cost per sq m" (or "cost per sq ft") measure of total building costs for a finished house (not including land costs). Most green home creators, builders, and architects will be able to give you this. But check how and when this was calculated. What date was the house finished? Is this the final costs plus all the extras? How was the house built? Was it by a builder or was some or all of it built by the owner via self-build (which will produce considerable savings)?

The unit measure will vary considerably depending on the quality of the finishes, bathroom and kitchen units installed, and solar systems fitted. But, adjusted to take account of inflation, this unit cost will give you a ball-park figure for a house of a certain size and finish, built in a certain way. It is also worth asking how much over budget the final costs were, and why. Almost all budgets are exceeded, so add on a good contingency sum for unforeseen extras. Armed with this, you can scale down your dream fantasy to a more real house in a real world.

Funding an ecological house may present problems, so start researching this early, too. Traditionally, most mortgage companies are conservative and only finance fairly conventional houses constructed of familiar materials. So, if you are planning on an unusual design built of unconventional materials, expect to spend more time finding the right funder. Sometimes banks, especially ethically motivated ones, are more open to environmental projects. As a last resort, where all else has failed, a specialist ecological building society or funding group may come to the rescue.

From brief to sketch design

Your early work on concepts and ideas will be invaluable as you begin to talk to your architect. Your architect will discuss their feasibility and may advise modifications. These will all be built into a written client brief, which should include your aims, design-style preferences, ecological/healthy design requirements, space functions and facilities, budget, schedule, and who will be responsible for decisions and payment as the project proceeds.

Next come sketch schemes or outline proposals showing the basic house design on the site. Make sure you like and understand these, and ask for some perspectives or three-dimensional images to help. Pin them up and look at them every day, talk about them with your partner and family, show them to craftspeople you hope to use, ask for comments and jot them down on a pad kept beside the plans. Discuss these with the architect and if you are not happy, ask for revisions. John and Nancy (see pp. 134–9) found the costs were too high for their original design, so the architect reduced the size without losing the basic concept.

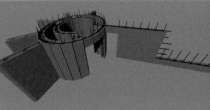

Architect Craig Henritzy's computer-aided vision for SunHawk (left), and the "Rastra" construction system diagram (below).

Planning approval

When you have agreed the outline design, it will be used, plus details of exterior materials, to apply for planning permission. You may encounter some stumbling blocks here for ecological houses, especially in densely built towns or areas of special architectural interest. These may be: solar panels on roofs, turf roofs, wind turbines, unusual design styles, exterior materials unfamiliar to the area, or even large areas of glazing, such as passive solar windows and conservatories/sunspaces. A lot depends on how overlooked the house will be, whether there are objections from adjacent owners, and the eco-experience and attitude of local planners.

Revisions and negotiations usually bring a solution. But sometimes planners can be resistant, so it is best to talk to them at the outset to find out current policies on sustainable building. To overcome this in sensitive locations, it is better if you acquire a site where the rear of the property can be sun-facing, so solar panels, sunspaces, and passive solar windows are unseen from the street frontage. Another advantage is that this should allow for a more imaginative and unconventional design style at the rear, as long as the street façade is compatible with the area.

From working drawings to contract

Once planning approval has been granted, the architect will produce working drawings showing the detailed construction. These will be sent for building regulations (codes) approval. New materials can cause hitches, as architect Darrel DeBoer (see pp. 120–5) found when his straw-bale designs met some opposition. Later after much discussion, he was asked to help rewrite the county's straw-bale codes.

A building specification itemizing all materials and works is now produced. Check that the architect has included all the sustainable and healthy building items you originally discussed. If the structure requires complicated structural "calculations", the architect will advise the use of a consultant civil engineer. If you want the main builder to use a particular contractor to do part of the work – say, solar-panel installation or hand-build kitchen cabinets – then these will become "nominated subcontractors". The working drawings, specification, and schedule are then sent out to tender to a selected list of "approved contractors" that needs to be agreed with you. Each item in the specification is priced and a total sum given for the job. The builders will confirm, or otherwise, if they can meet the contract schedule. After the tenders have been returned, the architect will advise you on the one you should accept or seek to negotiate. Finally, the architect will prepare a building contract (using one of the standard forms) and arrange for it to be signed by you and the chosen builder. Remember, the building contract is an agreement between you (not the architect) and the builder, so check it over carefully before signing.

Architect Jeff Gold's drawing of the East elevation for the Funk Homestead (above).

5 HUT EARTHSHIP

Earthships symbolize independence and self-reliance. Often off-grid, drawing power from the sun and wind, and water from rain and snow, they are built of natural and recycled materials, and reuse and treat their own wastewater. Fun to live in and organically shaped, they are now designed for modular self-build and package building.

Account of author's stay in an Earthship

Ever since I first learned about Mike Reynolds and his "Earthships", I had been intrigued and wanted to know more about them. What exactly were they? What was it like to live in one? The opportunity to find out came during a recent visit to New Mexico when I found that it was possible for my wife Joss and I to stay in a guest rental unit called The Hut Earthship.

It was a spectacular journey from Taos over the rolling sage-covered mesa with its breathtaking backdrop of the Sangre de Cristo Mountains — and across the dramatic deep gorge of the Rio Grande river. Still acclimatizing to the 2,075m (6,800ft) altitude and the dry, windy, high-desert conditions, we arrived exhilarated, and a little breathless, at the organically shaped Earthship Biotecture office.

We were met by Hillary, who, after showing us around the visitor display, guided us to our destination — The Hut. She told us that the whole Earthship subdivision, known as the Greater World Earthship Community, was started in 1994 and now covers 255 hectares (630 acres). She gave us a tour explaining that the 93 sq m (1,000 sq ft) house was built in 2000 to one of the newest Earthship designs. This has a long, south-facing internal greenhouse connected to two domed, circular spaces — one for the living room, one for the double bedroom.

The large greenhouse contains the kitchen and a verdant raised planter with banana trees, from which Hillary informed us "guests can often pick their own fresh bananas". It also served to treat kitchen and bathroom greywater before it is used to flush the toilet. She told us that the house was off-grid and showed us the electrical system, which used solar electricity from photovoltaic panels on the roof. This electricity is used as DC current to power special 12V equipment, such as the super-insulated DC refrigerator, satellite television, and some 12V lighting, and AC current (converted via an "inverter") for items that need more power, and some of the lights. "Please

The sun-facing living space can be seen from this view (above left), with solar panels and greenhouse windows making the most of the sunshine.

The roofscape is designed to catch every drop of rain (left), and the domed living and sleeping spaces have ventilating skylights

The circular stone-floored living space with a fabric tent inner ceiling and rustic tree marking the entrance to the kitchen/dining area (opposite).

A domed, circular sleeping space with a Mexican-style adobe screen wall (left), decorated with a mirror and recycled bottles.

switch off the inverter at night or when you leave for the day," she asked "to conserve power." So, after showing us some other features, such as the constant solar hot water in the shower, and the separate drinking water spigot to be used for cooking and teeth cleaning, she departed.

Although it was a fresh and windy October evening outside, the interior felt invitingly warm and peaceful. The setting sun filtered through the banana trees and filled the space with light and shadows. In fact, if anything, the interior felt a little stuffy, since nobody had recently lived in the house. This, however, was simply remedied by opening a vent window in the greenhouse and skylights at the top of the domed living room and bedroom to "flush out" the warm air. These were manually operated. By pulling a dangling rope through its cleats, the counterweighted skylights opened upward.

The sturdy, solid-wood kitchen units had unusual, beaten-copper inlay panels (cut from scraps from a local copper mill). Having stored our food in the "Sunfrost" high-efficiency refrigerator, supper was cooked on a propane gas oven (an electric appliance would be too much of a drain on the solar power system) and eaten off a built-in dining table partly supported by a rustic tree post. We saved our food scraps for Hillary's chickens since The Hut had no compost arrangement. We put all cans, bottles, and card into the recycling bin, from where they would be sorted and used as materials to build other Earthships.

Relaxing in the living room, I thought I'd try the somewhat incongruous satellite television. Even though it offered hundreds of channels, it was more entertaining to sample the Earthship videos that showed how to build your own.

The water being really hot suggested a luxurious bath in the organic tile and stone-slab tub. A generous-sized double bed located in the middle of the round bedroom rested, Mexican-fashion, on a solid podium. A stylish adobe screen wall at its head was decorated with a mirror and embedded recycled bottles. Lying in bed we could look upward and see the stars through the skylight. And what stars they were! The air being so pure and clear here, it was possible to see an amazing display, including the Milky Way arching clearly overhead. Added to this, there was a full moon and during the night we awoke to see her through the bedroom skylight moving slowly across the sky.

The next morning, we explored the area and saw other Earthship groups that gave us an idea of what the community may be like when more fully developed. Some were split-level, some were duplexes, and a few were offices. They mainly receded into the ground, and when seen from the rear they were lost to view in the desert scrub. One Earthship in the process of being built had half-completed, U-shaped, load-bearing walls built of used car tyres filled with rammed earth – alternative designs are now available in straw bale, concrete and adobe. Partition walls incorporated used cans and glass bottles, and many of the components are prefabricated off-site to make assembly easier and quicker.

Earthship Biotecture now offers a "Packaged Earthship" and often builds "shell and systems" options. This allows the owner to reduce costs by completing the interior. A typical two-bedroomed package would provide a finished exterior with all systems functioning, including systems such as rainwater "catch", grey- and blackwater sewage, and all plumbing. AC and DC power is provided by the prebuilt Power Organizing Module (POM), solar panel array, and optional wind turbine. But all of the interior work, including the floors, ceilings, partitions, cabinets, doors, and plaster, is left for the owner, or the owner's craftspeople, to finish off.

The organic design of the Earthship is taken through to the details – such as this solar-powered porch light above a small peep window beside the front door (right).

Returning to The Hut that evening, we read the entries in the guest book. They were almost all complimentary, and here are a just couple:

"This place is as close to Nature as you can get without camping . . . what a great concept this is for intelligent and compassionate living."
Peace, Lesley NYC

"We have come to see it . . . now we will build it."
Eve and Natalie, San Luis Obispo, CA

So, on our last night in The Hut we also made our entry in the book. We were sorry to leave the next day; we had already become fond of life in an Earthship. As I left, I recalled the words of Mike Reynolds: "We will have time to think of each other and the planet. Peace on Earth will no longer be a dream, it will simply be a result of the way we live."

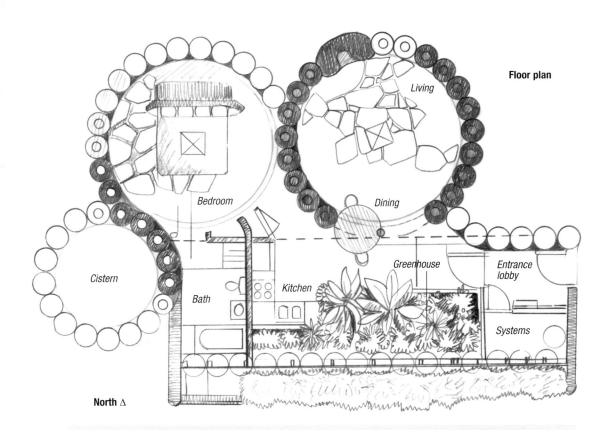

Floor plan

Living

Bedroom

Dining

Cistern

Greenhouse

Entrance
lobby

Bath

Kitchen

Systems

North △

eco data

CONSTRUCTION
• Earth-rammed tyre "brick" load-bearing walls, insulated
• Recycled aluminium cans and glass bottles partition walls
• Ply roof trusses and timber "greenhouse" frame

MATERIALS
• Used car tyres, cans, and bottles
• Cement and adobe plaster
• Salvaged or sustainably sourced timber
• Double-pane insulated windows
• Metal roof decking

SOFT ENERGY SYSTEM
• 2.5–8kW photovoltaic panels (120w modules)
• POM (Power Organizing Module) and batteries
• Optional wind turbine

HEATING
• Earth berm and insulation reduces demand
• Passive solar gain via "greenhouse"
• Massive thermal mass in walls stores energy
• Thermal window shades retain warmth at night
• Back-up fireplace

COOLING
• Roof and wall insulation, earth berm and earth-linking help maintain stable temperatures
• Passive ventilation via low window vents and roof skylights

WATER
• Rainwater stored in two or more 22,750 litre (5,000 gallon) cisterns
• Solar water system with back-up gas water heating
• Treated greywater for toilet flushing
• Blackwater treatment via solar septic tank, filters, and plants

LANDSCAPE
• Internal and external planters

CHAPTER 5

building it

Building with earth bags at a CalEarth workshop (above).

The "greenhouse" timber framework of a partially completed Earthship (opposite).

Building is a basic human skill. Our ancestors would have built their own houses, as do many people around the world today, especially in the developing world. Deep within most of us is the desire to build something. So, if the urge is strong within you, by all means let this energy and enthusiasm have its head.

There is little else that is so satisfying as building your own home. But do be realistic about what you can handle. If you are a first-time builder, you really ought to sign up for some building courses and hands-on workshops in the "green" materials you plan to use. You could also cut your teeth on a small backyard project built of the planned materials – a sort of microcosm of the larger house. Then you will be able to assess more realistically your capabilities – your health, age, strength, and manual dexterity. You may find you have a natural affinity with, or a dislike of, certain skills, and this will guide you to the ones to take on personally and the ones to farm out to others.

The most important thing to assess is the amount of free time you have. Building jobs take a long time – usually far longer than you first expect. Bad weather, hold-ups with supplies, wrong materials' deliveries, subcontractor delays, problems and disputes, and site accidents are just some of the delaying factors. So if you are to

play a major part in the process, you will need a lot of uninterrupted free time. Some self-builders try to fit house-building around their paid work and use every available moment in their evenings, weekends, and vacations to finish the house. This can be very stressful for all concerned.

Consider carefully the order of the work and how to minimize its impact on your family. Where are you and the family going to live while the new house is being built? For financial reasons, this may mean selling your present home to fund the building work. If so, you might be able to stay with friends or family or consider living in a caravan (trailer) near by, or on site. But make this as brief as possible – the initial novelty soon wears off. If you are renovating an existing house that needs a major overhaul, try to complete one room at a time so they can be used as havens from the general mess and confusion. It is easy to become overwhelmed and dispirited living in a long-term building site and you need somewhere to get away and recoup.

If you are building a new house, start on the foundations and exterior work in the spring and try to complete the building shell – roof, walls, and windows – plus utility connections, by the time winter sets in. Then you can move inside and concentrate on the interior in a relatively safe and protected environment.

Project management

"On budget and on schedule" are the magic words you hope to hear throughout a well-run building process. However, even with the best-laid plans, it is all too rare that you will hear them uttered.

Despite this, good project management will make all the difference between success and disaster. If you are employing an architect, clarify who will be responsible for project management. For single houses, the main contractor is often expected to fulfil this day-to-day function, with the architect inspecting the work on a weekly basis, and when a critical building operation is about to commence, such as laying foundations, for example. But if you want more intensive project management, you could consider hiring a professional project manager to take over from the architect when the building starts on site.

A project manager will coordinate the main contractor's work with that of the subcontractors and suppliers, and will ensure that all statutory site inspections are made and building approvals obtained for completed work. Adherence to contract drawings, priced specifications, and agreed schedule will all be monitored on a daily basis and any variations agreed with you in advance. Regular site meetings should be held to assess progress, problems, and remedial actions. If you cannot for some reason be part of these, ask to see the meeting minutes and arrange your own weekly meetings with the project manager to keep abreast of developments. Sarah and James (see pp. 40–5) felt a project manager for their cohousing project would have been helpful.

Kits and packages

To avoid the problems of building your own home from scratch, kit homes and packages are available. The idea is that by standardizing materials and pre-assembling them into large components in the factory, on-site building work is kept to a minimum and is much faster than conventional house-building. By reducing site work, project management is simpler and more straightforward, too. Kit house companies usually have their own team to handle and manage delivery, site preparation, foundations, and assembly. The service can be fine or it can be

Could you be a project manager?

Much depends on the size and complexity of the project as well as your determination, knowledge, experience, and time. Only take on something small and simple if you are new to the game. But if you feel you know what you are doing, are strong on organization and coordination, can manage people, deal with finances, be a problem-solver, and have plenty of time to spare, you could make a good candidate.

Assuming you have production drawings, specifications with budget estimates, start and finish dates, adequate finance and approvals, the critical preparatory items to cover include:

• Compile a detailed construction schedule using a simple bar chart or computer software showing start and finish dates for all major tasks and materials needed. Be aware that for some tasks (and subcontractors) to start, others will have to be completed first. Tracing these throughout the schedule will give a "critical path" to be maintained so delays are minimized. Expect to have to update this on a regular basis.

• Create a cash-flow spreadsheet showing the timing of all anticipated expenditures and inputs of your finance to ensure the project does not grind to a halt due to lack of funds at any point. Spreadsheet and specialist self-build software will help. Keep your budget costs (as per your original specification) as your baseline so you can compare actual costs against budget and keep track of extras. You will also need to keep detailed financial records of invoice payments, wages, and all administration costs. At least keep all bills and receipts in one place.

• Make a site plan showing boundary fencing, delivery area, materials' stores, site office, toilets, waste collection/recycling area, and ensure basic utilities are connected and that all health and safety requirements and insurances are in place.

Still keen to take it on? If so, read on.

disappointing. Check out the experiences of other clients before choosing a kit.

To be in more control, you can do part or all of the work yourself, or use a builder. An example is a packaged Earthship (see pp. 64–9), where a range of predesigned options is available depending on a client's needs, budget, self-build inclinations, and capacity. Log homes and timber chalets are other popular kit homes. But kits have come a long way and now offer a surprising variety of styles, customized layouts, and special features. You should certainly look into these when researching your natural home.

Building the timber frame – the ultimate kit house (above).

At last, after months of preparation, the time comes to make a start on the building work on site. If you are acting as "boss" then you will have to deal with initiating and coordinating everything. There is not enough space here to cover in detail all the matters you need to know about being a builder – this would take a book in itself. But, here are some important areas you need to think about:

Building team

Who will do the work? Will you form a core team or crew to work with? Will it have a mix of trade skills or will you use trades in sequence – carpenter, plumber, electrician, and plasterer? Or, will you hire trades to work as subcontractors? You might find that the work is too much for you to cope with by yourself, or that you are going too slowly to keep up with the schedule. Dan (see pp. 52–7) built the first floor, called in help to finish the second floor and roof, and then took over again to finish off.

Hiring subcontractors

Alongside the work you and your team do, expect to have to subcontract some work out to others. This can be for anything you want, from bricklaying and plastering to plumbing and roofing. For natural building, this may also include specialists who have experience with using "green" materials and ecosystems, such as solar power or water recycling. You can hire your selected craftspeople in this way, too. Always obtain references, obtain competitive quotes, and place a written order stating clearly the work involved, the agreed price, and the date by which it is to be done.

Plant and tools

It is worth investing in the best tools you can afford. After all, they are going to be your trusty friends for a long time! Good-quality tools last longer and are easier to use. Battery-powered tools are much more convenient and safer to use as they avoid dangers of tripping over and accidentally cutting electric cables. In the long run, it may be better to buy them and sell them on completion rather than hiring them. But if the investment is too large, buy some and hire others, such as heavy plant and equipment – earth diggers, cranes, transformers, and scaffolding. If hiring equipment, ensure that you have it on site only when required, not hanging around unused clocking up extra charges.

Supplies

You will need to organize the supply of materials to the site. This will involve competitive quotes from different suppliers, opening accounts, and negotiating discounted prices based on the size of your order. Where possible, order direct from the factory to save costs. Prompt payment can also gain a further discount. Make sure to agree account payment terms or the supplier may demand cash on delivery. Go through the same vetting and order-placing routines as with sub-contractors, and decide who has the authority to place orders. Check deliveries against the orders as they arrive and notify the supplier immediately of any discrepancies or damaged items. Log all deliveries and file orders and delivery notes.

Safety

Building sites are dangerous places and accidents will happen. Falls from ladders and scaffolding, collapsed trench shoring, objects falling from a height, cuts from saws and drills, and bruises from hammers are some common accidents. Keep the site tidy and dispose of rubbish frequently. Wear protective clothing, including hard hats and stout boots (not trainers) with strong toe caps and soles to prevent nails puncturing your foot; wear a mask and goggles to protect against dust and gloves to protect against preservatives and splinters in wood. Keep a first-aid box and an accident logbook, and display safety information clearly on site. Resist taking short cuts, follow manufacturers' instructions, be careful at all times and, hopefully, you will have a safe and happy site.

Building in progress at the Shenoa Retreat (above).

Supervision and control

Contact the local authority building department to find out the key stages where they will want to come and inspect work as it proceeds. It is always best to maintain good working relations with building inspectors. Some "green" materials may be unfamiliar to them and you will have to provide extra information and samples for approval. This can hold up work, so it is better to have an early meeting to go over any unusual materials and construction methods.

If an architect has been employed to supervise the work on site, he or she will visit the site to inspect the construction works and advise on any technical problems. Otherwise, if you are supervising the work, make sure that subcontractors know you are the "boss" and have the power to approve or reject work. And, make doubly certain that you have received all approvals and subcontractor certificates confirming compliance of their work with current regulations (codcs). You will need these to have the house insured once completed, and to show potential buyers if you decide to sell.

Completion

Finally, when the house is completed, you will need to:

• Gather together all formal approvals and certifications – legal, planning, building inspector, electrical, water, plumbing systems, and so on. If you have used an architect, he or she will issue a certificate of practical completion that confirms that the house has been constructed in accordance with all the approved drawings and specifications.

• Have the utility services connected.

• Arrange for house insurance.

• Set up maintenance routines.

Then, celebrate with a house-warming party!

6 GREEN CONDO

Outstanding for urban chic and style, this project combines new build and renovation to provide affordability and modern ecoliving in the heart of downtown Berkeley. Found objects create a light-hearted theme, from windscreen stair rails to signboard fencing, while passive solar gain and high insulation reduce heating and cooling needs.

The site of this project is absolutely ideal for an ecological development. With its central location within walking distance of downtown Berkeley and the university campus, it is not only within a block of the local bicycle lane network, it is also adjacent to two bus routes and a short walk to two local BART (Bay Area Rapid Transit) stations.

The nine-unit "green" condo compound, which was designed for owner occupation, came to life in two phases. The first was a renovation project and the second was a new-build project. The credit for this stylishly modern and well-designed project goes to local Berkeley eco-architects Karl Wanaselja and Cate Leger, who not only managed to raise the necessary funds, but also found the site, made the plans, obtained all the necessary permissions, and helped construct the buildings.

They were helped throughout the project by design-build practitioners Frederick Hyer and Scott McGlashan.

Phase One – Renovation

The first phase was to renovate and convert an early 1900s corner grocery store with two upper apartments that had long been underused and neglected. The new scheme kept the two upstairs apartments and divided the downstairs commercial space into two. "All have ingenious floor plans," explains Cate, "which, although compact, are ultra-functional to take maximum advantage of the existing building envelope."

Newly installed oversized windows and skylights ensure that the apartments are filled with natural light and make the best use of solar gain. High-vented ceilings help keep the rooms cool in summer. The most engaging and fun architectural features of the project also make memorable ecological statements. One example of this is the imaginative reuse of aluminium street signs. Once sanded, they were hung on the outside of the building to make perfect siding (cladding). Some of the old signs, with their street names still visible, are used elsewhere for decorative

The first phase of the development was the renovation of a former corner shop to create four apartments (left). The second phase (opposite) was a new-build infill apartment block.

fences. Disused car parts are employed with great panache throughout. "Karl took trips to some 'pick-and-pull' car dumps," smiled Cate, "and just selected what he needed. It's amazing what you can find there!"

Salvaged Mazda and Porsche hatchback windows serve as glass awnings over exterior doors, while Volvo hatchback versions provide stylish internal staircase railings. In bathrooms, smaller car windows make convenient shelves. Other salvaged materials, including old-growth Douglas fir and redwood from the original building, were reused to make window sills, build new walls, patch floors, and create custom doors. Most of the old doors and their door jambs were retained or reused – even the 100-year-old timber laths, exposed when wall plaster was removed, were renovated to make the interior richer. Every effort was made to use nontoxic materials and finishes. All paints were low- or non-VOC types. No PVC, toxic adhesives, or treated wood were used at all. Instead, all woodwork plus the original fir floors, was finished with natural oils and waxes – any carpeting laid was natural wool.

Phase Two

An open-plan kitchen/dining area in a Phase Two apartment (above).

Detail of car window rail supports (right).

Reclaimed glass car windows make feature stair rails (far right), here looking down from the landing.

Energy-efficiency was a priority. The roof and all external walls were insulated with cellulose insulation made from recycled newspapers. All single-pane windows were replaced with double-pane, argon-filled, low-emissivity units. Only high-efficiency or "Energy Star" appliances were installed in the apartments. To minimize on-grid electricity, high levels of natural daylight reduce dependence on electric lights, and rooftop photo-voltaic panels supply some off-grid supplies.

This dish-shaped key holder at the top of the entrance stairs (left) ensures keys are always conveniently to hand.

Phase One

West elevation

Architect's drawing (above) of the west elevation showing Phase One (on the right) and Phase Two (on the left). Note the linking "mews" between the two phases and small residents' garden.

eco data

CONSTRUCTION
- Sustainably harvested timber frame clad in salvaged aluminium siding
- Reuse of existing structure in Phase One
- All concrete contains 50% fly ash
- Low-emissivity windows and external doors
- Floors finished with poured concrete tinted with natural dyes

MATERIALS
- Salvaged street signs for fences and gates
- Reclaimed car windows and doors for gates, awnings, stair rails, and shelves
- Salvaged Douglas fir window sills and redwood flooring
- Terrazzo kitchen counters made of recycled glass/concrete mix
- Non-VOC paints and nontoxic adhesives
- Natural oil or wax finishes
- Plaster-only finishes to internal walls

SOFT ENERGY SYSTEMS
- 1kW photovoltaic system interlinked with city electricity grid
- Energy-saving appliances
- Operable skylights enhance natural lighting and reduce need for artificial light

HEATING
- Blown cellulose insulation from recycled paper reduces need
- Passive solar gain via south-facing windows
- High-efficiency forced-air units (rarely needed)
- 136 litre (30 gallon) hot-water heaters located close to point of use

COOLING
- High insulation levels reduce need
- Natural ventilation via windows, skylights, and roof vents

LANDSCAPE
- Small footprint of project and use of urban infill site
- Small resident garden
- Rainwater returned to site via soakaways (drywells) and permeable paving composed of decomposed granite
- Native planting and drought-tolerant species, irrigation system not necessary. Only occasional summer watering needed after first year when plants are established

ground floor here rather than a residential unit. Responding to local climate and site conditions, the north side was designed to be more enclosed with smaller windows, and lower room heights, while the south-facing living rooms had windows high in the wall to catch the sunlight and bring it deep into the building in winter. The exterior decks are wide enough to encourage outdoor living and are warm even on a winter day. In fact, this new project, with its four two-bedroomed units and commercial unit, is one of the first, small, "green", mixed-use developments in Berkeley.

Similar to Phase One, the units have small, well laid-out, and efficient floor plans. There is no wasted space and none is inaccessible. The 5 x 15cm (2 x 6in) sustainably harvested timber framing and 35cm (14in) ceiling space are both super-insulated with blown-in cellulose material. All concrete contains 50 per cent fly ash (a waste product of coal burning). As with Phase One, the building is fitted out with low-emissivity windows and salvaged, sustainable, resource-efficient, and nontoxic materials.

Except for the bathrooms, units are plastered only, largely eliminating the need for paint, trim, and caulking. Xantha, one of the first owners, says: "The place is so well insulated, I've never needed to use the heating since I've been here." As in Phase One, used car windows act as railings, awnings, and shelves, but this time, two rows of old Volvo hatchback doors have been welded together to make a rather unexpected, yet entirely functional, spacious entry gate to the bike and car-parking area.

Other unusual eco-features include glass terrazzo kitchen counters using recycled glass, unique, hand-blown light fixtures, and striking concrete floor patterns. Karl scored and stained all of the finished concrete floors in beautiful Mondrian-like patterns, obviating any aesthetic need for floor coverings. These mark the floor area, where sunshine falls through a nearby window at different times of the day on Cate's birthday.

Phase Two – New Building

Making the best use of the available site, the new block was sited east-west, just behind Phase One, so the new apartments could take advantage of a southerly aspect. This also meant that only one narrow side of the block needed to be exposed to the busy street. As further protection, a commercial space was sited on the

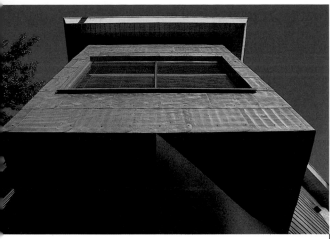

The striking design of a bay window in the Phase Two development (opposite).

Looking up from the street at corner bay in Phase One (left).

An external stairway leading up to the terrace and entry to the Phase Two apartments (below).

Landscape

A 3.5m (11ft) wide courtyard, or "mews", that joins the new block and the renovated building, acts as an entrance to the new units and small garden for all the residents. The mews and north side of the building are planted with shade-loving species, while the sunnier areas feature drought-tolerant plants. A drainage swale along the north edge of the property catches rainwater and is planted with red alders and other riparian species. Permeable paving of light golden-coloured decomposed granite in the parking area, bricks in the mews, and three soakaways (drywells) help rain to percolate into the soil and keep all rainwater from running off the site. The drought-tolerant plants need no irrigation system, other than occasional summer watering, once they are established.

This impressive project shows how good, sustainable design can be combined with exciting, modern architecture. As Xantha says, "I love it here, it's so comfortable and well designed. Being so central and close to everything, it's easy to walk, bike, or take BART instead of always using a car. And, while it's small, it feels spacious, and is very easy to maintain. It also looks super cool while being both functional and efficient!"

designing with natural systems

Using the natural power of the sun, wind, water, and earth is one of the great delights of a natural home. It puts you in touch with nature and constantly reminds you that your home is part of a much larger ecosystem.

Our homes are significant contributors to global warming and climate change. Conventional heating and cooling systems that burn fossil fuels – gas, coal, wood, and oil – all produce carbon dioxide, one of the main contributors to global warming. But we are surrounded by free, benign energy that can be used to heat and cool our homes. Sun, wind, and water, as well as the earth itself, all provide more than enough power to meet our needs. Solar energy can bring warmth into the house and also be harnessed to produce electricity and hot water. Wind can cool houses, pump water from wells and power generators to make electricity. Water can bring humidity to help cooling in dry climates and electricity via hydropower. The earth offers us protection from the cold and a stable ambient underground temperature that can be tapped into to provide heat or cooling. The key is to work with nature, understand the principles of each, and how they work together. Use these life-giving natural elements as inspirations for your design.

Designing with the sun

We have always responded to the power of the sun and its daily and seasonal cycles. Today, once again, we are rediscovering how solar power can change our lives.

Start by looking at the site of your new home or location of your existing one. Ideally you want a south-facing site with protection to the north. For maximum passive solar gain, the solar aspect needs to be as unrestricted as possible. Orientate the layout of your house to make full use of this, or adapt your existing house by increasing the window area or adding a solar sunspace. Next, build using a high level of thermal mass and plenty of insulation to the walls, roof, and ground floor. For more protection from cold winds, plant a windbreak of evergreen trees and bushes or mound up an earth-berm. For a new house, consider building the exposed rear of the house into the ground or covering the roof with earth.

Having created your basic solar-house design, you can consider whether you need "back-up" heating or cooling. Bear in mind that many of the back-up heating systems installed in the featured homes in this book were rarely needed. Few had any mechanical cooling system and, if they did, it was solar powered.

Solar water panels at the
Funk Homestead (above)
provide free hot water,
courtesy of the sun.

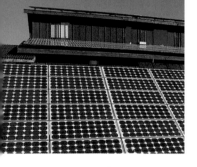

New and recycled photovoltaic (PV) panels at SunHawk's barn (above and top), which houses batteries and equipment.

Photovoltaics (PV)

The solar cell is the miniature masterpiece that converts sunlight directly into electricity. When these cells are wired together in series they make a PV "module". Lightweight modules of 36 or 72 cells, producing between 18 and 24 volts, are a fairly common in domestic installations. When these modules are connected and wired together, they form an "array". Currently, there are four commercial types: single crystalline, poly-crystalline, string ribbon, and amorphous, or thin film. You will need to get technical advice on which is best for your particular needs.

There are also roof tile modules. These have the advantage of integrating seamlessly into the surrounding roof tiling rather than having to be mounted on top, as is the case with conventional arrays. But, with space, you can locate the arrays away from the house and mount them on tracker poles (an Earthship option), on a barn roof (Funk Homestead), or next to a barn (SunHawk). To complete your PV system, you can opt for a utility "intertie" or "net metering" system – you feed any excess PV power to the electricity company and buy it back when you have a deficit. Or, you can opt for a battery-storage system with or without an "inverter" to covert DC to AC current, or for a combination of intertie and battery storage. Grants (tax credits) are available to help with component and installation costs.

Green electricity

If you do not have a PV system, you can still benefit from "green" electricity. This is electricity sold by utility companies that is produced without the use of fossil fuels. Wind farms and large-array PV installations are the main sources, plus wave power and hydropower. Remember, though, that some large-scale hydroelectricity projects have damaged the environment and there is a certain amount of opposition to land-based wind farms in some areas. There may be a small extra "green tariff" on the unit price, but if you are happy with the sources and the price, sign up.

Design with water

Water is life. It brings fertility and regeneration to the planet and health and rejuvenation to the body and soul. Water is one of our most precious resources and should be conserved and used wisely. As well as incorporating water-conserving systems in the home, let its spiritual and health-giving energies inspire your designs. The Japanese-style "rain chains" at Econest (see pp. 104–9), the secret spring and grotto at SunHawk (see pp. 134–9), the path-side rills at Springfield Cohousing (see pp. 40–5), and the water basin in the porch of Orchard House (see pp. 120–5) are all simple ways to express this love of water.

Rainwater saving

On the practical side, a rain-harvesting system can range from the simplest garden water butt to a full-blown water-catchment system. In an Earthship (see pp. 64–9), the metal roof and gutters carry rain and snow melt to the two ends of the building, where it is filtered and stored in cisterns. The cisterns are buried in an earth berm to prevent freezing, maintain a stable temperature, and reduce algal growth. The water is used to irrigate indoor and outdoor planting and, after more filtering, for bathroom use.

Groundwater

Many places have a problem with dwindling water tables, and so the more rainwater that can be returned to the ground the better. Instead of draining run-off from your house into a sewer system, allow it to soak back into the ground. Green Condo (see pp. 76–81) has a simple "drywell" system to do this. Springfield Cohousing has its "SUDS" design, and Econest roofs their rain-chains and irrigation network.

Greywater

Water that has been used in the kitchen and for washing in the bathroom is called "greywater". In a conventional domestic plumbing system, once used it would be consigned to the sewer. In a natural home, however, it is cleansed and recycled.

In an Earthship greywater is passed through filters and is then cleansed via a long pathway through indoor "planters" lined with pumice, sand, and plastic. This recycled water is stored separately ready to flush toilets, completely eliminating the need to use fresh water for this. The water flushed from the toilet is called "blackwater".

Blackwater

"Low-flush" toilets are now on the market that are very water-efficient, but to use no water at all, install a compost toilet. Modern versions are safe, hygienic, and odourless. But blackwater can be treated, too. Earthships do this using a special solar septic tank that accelerates the anaerobic process. Finally, the blackwater passes through an outdoor lined planter with layers of gravel, pumice, soil, and roots.

Approvals

Check on water and plumbing regulations (codes), as approvals may be necessary, if not essential.

A rain chain and square catchment pond (above left) at Econest, and a chodzu-bachi water feature (above) at Orchard House.

Solar hot water

Solar water heating may be expensive to install, but it has a long life expectancy and almost no running costs. In the long term it is one of the lowest cost options available to heat water. A typical system has a "flat-plate collector panel" – a thin, glass-covered box containing piping snaking to and fro over an insulated black surface – a heat-exchanger, pump, hot water tank, and controls. The piping is filled with an anti-freeze fluid, which heats up as it passes through the collector panel. This heat is then transferred to the domestic water supply via the heat-exchanger, and the resulting hot water stored in an insulated storage tank ready for later use.

This solar hot-water system can be used either to provide hot water totally or, in less sunny weather or in more temperate climates, to heat water partially for a final boost from a conventional water-heating system. The collector panels can be roof-mounted or located elsewhere conveniently close to the house.

Radiant floor heating

Another benefit of solar water heating is that you can use it to heat the house. By using the same hypocaust principle the ancient Romans installed in their homes and *thermae* (public baths), the heat can be used under the floors of your home.

Radiant underfloor heating is a popular choice in a number of the homes featured in this book as it gives a gentle, unobtrusive warmth that spreads evenly throughout the whole space – the "healthy-house" radiant heating much favoured by practitioners of baubiologie (see p. 26). In addition, there are no radiators, air grilles, or visible pipes to get in the way. Instead, flexible underfloor piping is laid out in a convoluted pattern, much as in the "collector panel" above, over an insulated floor slab before the screed and floor finish are laid. Hot water, from the solar hot-water system (or other more conventional system) then circulates through the pipework to heat the room.

Photovoltaic (PV) and solar water panels (above) mounted on recycled rubber roof tiles at SunHawk.

Solar water panels and a small PV module (right) in the garden of Spiral House.

It is remarkable that in countries, from the Mediterranean to the Far East, simple rooftop solar water heaters have become endemic in houses, both rich and poor – a peaceful solar revolution that has spread around the world.

Water supply

Having your own water supply and so being independent of water companies can only be a dream for most people. Yet, with modern technology for those living in predominantly rural areas, it is not such an outlandish idea. If you have a spring or creek, natural pond, or well on your property, then you could be lucky. But first check if you have sole or shared rights to the water, and if there are any limiting conditions – only seasonal use or a maximum quantity of water that can be drawn off, for example. There may be a covenant in your property deeds.

Next, check with the local water authority to see what approvals or regulations are involved. Then have the water tested for quality and purity by an expert. It may look fine, but perhaps it is being polluted by a leak from a septic tank up the hill from you, or pesticide or artificial fertilizer run-off from an upstream farm.

Wells

The most common source of on-site domestic water is a well. A well is less likely than springs and ponds to be affected by surface pollution. Old well shafts were hand-dug and, therefore, tend to be quite wide and they may be surprisingly deep. Because of this, they are dangerous and there have been many instances of accidents involving people or animals falling down and drowning in them. They also seem to exert a particular fascination for children, so if you have an existing well on your land, make sure you cover the top with a strong, lockable lid.

A modern well has a narrow "driven", or drilled, 10 or 15cm (4 or 6in) diameter borehole encased in piping. An electric submersible pump with a draw-off pipe is then lowered to the bottom of the borehole. The pump can be driven by DC power from PV modules mounted at the wellhead or near by. Alternatively, you can use AC power from the grid. The water is pumped into a storage tank ready for use. Another system uses a wind-turbine-powered pump employing compressed air to lift the water.

A desert wind farm near Palm Springs, California, USA (above).

Wind power

You probably do not want to live where conditions are ideal for year-round wind power! Constant wind is unpleasant, especially in winter. And to be certain of having enough wind you will need to live in an exposed location or at a fairly high altitude. For most people, the best arrangement is to live in relatively sheltered locations and to opt for a "hybrid" solar/wind system. This is the ideal combination, as the two are complementary – solar power being best in summer; wind power being best in winter. Together, they offer improved reliability and a more cost-effective use of the same core system components.

Domestic wind turbines vary in size (diameter of their rotor blades) from "micro" 1–1.5m (3–5ft) to "mini" 1.5–2.75m (5–9ft) to "household-size" 3–7m (10–23ft) – the bigger the better for power generation.

Site a wind turbine well away from buildings, trees, and other wind obstructions, and mount it on a tall "tilt-up" tubular or lattice-steel tower. Power output increases with height and you need at least a 9m (30ft) tower for good performance. Micro turbine/tower kits are available for self-assembly, but for larger turbines, be on the safe side and use professionals to do the work.

Hydropower

If you are fortunate enough to have the right site, hydroelectricity is an attractive renewable energy choice. In ideal conditions, it can be cheaper than a PV system of comparable output.

So what is a good site? It all depends on water volume/weight and its fall, or "head". You can achieve the same output from a small volume of water falling a large distance as a large volume falling a small distance. The former situation – small spring/large fall – is better for your "micro-hydro" system as it will be smaller and cheaper to build. Find out if there are daily flow figures for the past 5–20 years available to check how dependable the supply is.

Apart from a site's potential energy output, other aspects may have to be considered, such as the effect on fish and aquatic wildlife, riparian rights, environmental conservation, recreation activities, land drainage, flood defence, trees, public access, and building control. Approach the local river authority early and seek their advice. You will probably need a licence from them anyway. Also check upstream obstructions and "abstractions" (diversion of water) or "impoundments" (a weir or sluice, for example). This may sound formidable, but if this is going to be your main source of power, you need to be certain it is feasible before you jump in and buy the land. In fact, the site of an old or disused water mill may well suit all these conditions and, if converted using modern equipment, can make an ideal hydropower project, and perhaps even double as your natural home too.

The basic parts are: supply pipeline ("penstock"), turbine, alternator/generator, regulator, wiring, and controls. With the constant output from hydropower, it is best to be grid-linked rather than having to use battery storage. If you are using hydropower in conjunction with PV and wind turbine, you can feed all sources into your central battery and DC/AC inverter/control units or, again, be grid-linked. There are different considerations for every site, so seek expert technical advice at the earliest possible stage.

A Tulikivi soapstone stove with bake oven (above) provides a central feature at Tesuque Econest.

warming. Support a tree-planting project to help counteract this, or if you have the available land, plant lots of trees.

Stoves

Traditional open-hearth fires may be attractive, but they are not the answer to today's heating needs due to their low efficiency and high emissions. Opt instead for the new range of clean-burn stoves that have been designed to be super-efficient by using catalytic methods to reduce emissions drastically. Many of these burn specially manufactured wood pellets, which is a wood by-product, at very high temperatures, thereby giving excellent heating and low emissions.

But if you are looking for something special that not only meets modern requirements, but is also visually beautiful and produces a long-lived and all-pervading warmth, then try a masonry stove. They can be hand-built by a local stove builder as was the case in Posts Standing (see pp. 14–19) or ordered from specialist companies. Used in northern mainland Europe for centuries, they are known as *kachelofen* (tile ovens) in German-speaking countries (where they double for cooking, too). However, the best-known and rightly famous are the Tulikivi stoves from Finland, as used in Econest and SunHawk (see pp. 104–9 and 134–9). They incorporate innovations such as "contraflow" and dual combustion to achieve very high efficiency.

With contraflow, the hot flue gases circulate up and down a long, convoluted flue within the heavy structure of the stove to allow the maximum time for the heat to be absorbed by the stone walls. The fireplace heats up quickly with one or two loads of firewood. This is sufficient to produce heat for the whole day in a properly insulated home. Made of silky smooth soapstone, these are the Rolls Royce of stoves. Although they are fairly costly to buy, you will never regret the investment as they are a real joy to own. Their gentle and healthy warmth gives your home a pleasant ambience that has to be experienced to be fully appreciated.

Back-up heating

If you have followed the basic principles of creating a solar home – sheltered from the worst of the weather and insulated to a very high standard – your need for supplementary heating will be significantly lowered, or even reduced virtually to nil. But many people still prefer to have some sort of secondary heating system to cope with unexpected cold snaps, to use occasionally for, say, social gatherings and parties, or as a back-up in emergencies.

Whatever back-up systems you choose, make sure it will run on renewable fuels, such as solar hot water for radiant floors, wood from properly managed sources, dead- or downwood, or wood by-products, such as wood pellets. Avoid using non-renewable fossil fuels, such as oil, gas, and coal. And make sure that your system is as thermally efficient and non-polluting as it possibly can be. But remember that no matter how efficient combustion appliances are, they still produce some carbon dioxide (and other combustion gases) that contribute to global

7 SPIRAL HOUSE

Adobe-style, straw-bale construction lent itself to flowing forms, giving rise to a home designed around the Golden Mean spiral form. And the round walls blended more comfortably with the meandering river-valley landscape. Passive solar gain, solar water heating, and rainwater collection strengthened the connection between landscape and building.

Travelling through New Mexico you grow used to a dry scrub landscape with views of distant mountains and mesas. So it's a surprise when you suddenly find yourself arriving in a lush green valley, woods and pastures set off with horses and grazing cattle. Called El Valle, and graced with the meandering Pecos River, it is no wonder that when Michael and Mahabba Kauffman first saw it they knew this was where they wanted to live. It was "pure serendipity", says Mahabba, when very soon they heard that some land was up for sale. The 13.5 hectares (33 acres) bordering the river was ideal, and they purchased it immediately.

House-building was not new to Michael, who, during a varied career as attorney, contractor, mediator, and more, had already built four houses. But this time the special beauty of the site called for something really creative and unique. This is when English-born Mahabba had an idea. In her work as an artist and potter, she had always been intrigued with spiral motifs, so why not make the new house in the form of a spiral?

Round walls, she felt, were much more natural and would blend more comfortably with the river-valley landscape. At first, Michael thought this would be too ambitious and would make too many practical construction difficulties. Then he remembered seeing how straw bales were being used and how it was fairly simple to build curved walls with them.

As Michael had not worked with straw-bale building before, he searched around for a specialist and found Turkish-born architect Erem Birkan, based in Santa Fe. Erem had perfected a new way of building load-bearing walls with straw bales, which he called "Baleblock". This combines the insulating value of straw with the structural strength of concrete. Using a special machine, standard straw bales are drilled with two 10cm (4in) holes and slotted over steel reinforcing bars set in the foundation. Once several layers have been stacked, the cavities are filled with concrete. These concrete pillars are then tied horizontally with concrete ring beams to create a solid post-and-beam structure.

The spiral form (above) is
evident as it rises up to the
domed meditation area at the
top of the house.

The entrance has a mosaic
pavement inset with the sacred
snake motif (right).

The seed of the spiral form for the house can be seen in this unusual terrazzo countertop in the heart of the kitchen (above), looking into the curved living area beyond.

But designing a spiral house was a challenge and Erem decided to work with his father, Sermet, a structural engineer in Turkey, and his architect brother, Arcan, on the more complicated design details of the building.

The final 260 sq m (2,800 sq ft) house plan was based on the ancient Golden Mean spiral – the spiral of natural growth. Starting on the ground floor, the hub is in the kitchen, the heart of the house. The spiral then flows outward around the entrance hall and living room and upward, via a curving staircase, to the master bedroom with its sun-wheel ceiling. Then it moves upward again, up another curved stair, to the top-floor circular meditation room surmounted by a wooden dome and central skylight of lotus-flower design.

The central, curving staircase walls are encased in local stonework using the traditional Pueblo Indian style of the Anasazi tribes. Local stone-masons were used for this and, in fact, only local craftspeople were employed on the project, even crafting the curved kitchen cabinets and hand-wrought ironwork. It was a community event.

Erem also introduced terrazzo (small pieces of marble mixed with tinted cement, ground smooth, and polished when dry) as the perfect material for pouring curved shapes for floors, stairs, kitchen worktops, and even the bathtub. Materials from recycled and renewable sources were used as much as possible. The "vigas" (traditional Mexican rustic roof beams) came from dead standing timber. Cork, a renewable resource, was laid as office flooring. The entrance door was purpose-made to fit stained glass – formerly part of a firescreen – found in the local flea market.

Passive solar design with large, sun-facing windows and heavy mass floors and internal walls catch and retain the sun's heat, while an earth berm and underground service rooms to the north protect and insulate the house in winter. Solar panels heat the domestic water, and may be used in future for radiant underfloor heating, which is presently provided by propane gas. Space is available to install the planned photo-voltaic electricity system. Heating via propane gas is rarely found to be needed due to the good

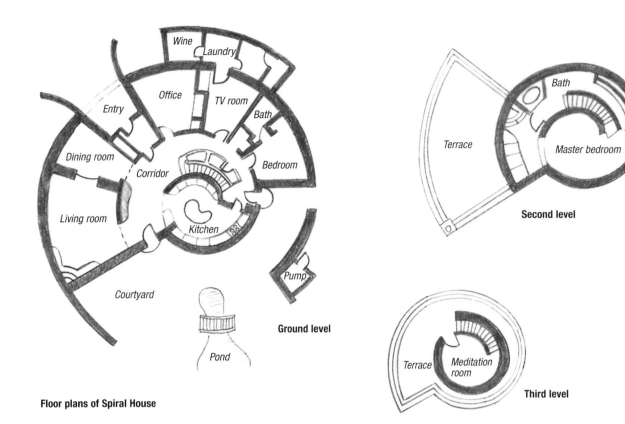

Wine
Laundry
Office
Entry
TV room
Bath
Dining room
Corridor
Bedroom
Living room
Kitchen
Courtyard
Pump
Ground level
Pond

Bath
Terrace
Master bedroom
Second level

Terrace
Meditation room
Third level

Floor plans of Spiral House

eco data

CONSTRUCTION
• "Baleblock" walls covered with earth/cement adobe
• Recycled vigas (peeled roof beams) from dead standing timber
• Recycled stone for fireplaces and stone facing to spiral stairway

MATERIALS
• Salvaged and recycled wood wherever possible
• New timber from sustainably harvested sources
• Renewable resources, such as cork flooring tiles
• Salvaged items, such as front door stained glass
• Local craftspeople employed

SOFT ENERGY SYSTEM
• Photovoltaic system to be installed shortly
• Service room ready to accommodate batteries, inverters, and so on

HEATING
• Passive solar design and good thermal mass in walls and floors
• Radiant floor heating powered by propane gas boiler (if needed)
• Back-up open fire in living room (if needed)

COOLING
• Earth-covered lower ground floors to help moderate temperature
• Massive walls help keep indoor temperature even
• Natural ventilation and "stack effect" via central stairwell to roof

WATER
• Solar water panels heat water
• Greywater and blackwater reedbed systems ready to be installed
• Rainwater harvested from roofs and stored in underground tanks

LANDSCAPE
• Permaculture garden and pond
• Stored rainwater irrigates land
• Plans for organic cooperative farm

insulation value of the straw-bale walls and the high thermal mass of the interior. The open fire in the living room is mainly decorative and is used mainly on festive occasions. Fortunately, as the temperature in summer rarely goes above 25°C (78°F) in the house, even though it may be 32°C (90°F) outside, artificial cooling is not required. Rainwater collected in large underground cisterns is used for the pond and watering the garden. Michael wants to go further and install a greywater system with reedbeds. Beyond this, his interest in permaculture has encouraged him to make plans to turn his land into a cooperative organic farm. Mahabba is keen to use the rich pasture to rear horses.

But not everything has gone smoothly. Although Erem originally advised on having metal sloping roofs, the Kauffmans wanted to have parapets to be in character with the local tradition of Santa Fe adobe. This meant that each of the three roof levels was flat and had to drain rainwater into the underground tanks via pipes built inside the straw-bale walls. Unfortunately, some of these became blocked and water permeated into the walls. To remedy the situation, large areas of straw bales had to be replaced, and the walls replastered and repainted. The lesson has been learned and Erem is definite that he would never again mix flat parapets and a straw-bale design.

Michael acted as construction manager, not only coordinating the work but also helping with the work on site himself. Because of this, he saved considerably on the overall cost. He also helped speed up the building process, which lasted only nine months, to save on the costs of subcontractors. But he estimates that building a complex, curved structure does have on-costs, maybe 20–30 per cent, as components have to fit more exactly and materials have to be flexible and/or flow to form curved shapes.

Now that it is all finished, and the teething problems are sorted out, the Kauffmans are delighted with their spiral-shaped home and are looking forward to a peaceful and sustainable future in their beautiful green valley.

The entrance hallway (left) with its stained-glass iris flower motifs and stairs curving upward, following the spiral movement of the house.

The domed and ribbed wooden ceiling (right) of the meditation room (below right).

The round master bedroom with its sunburst ceiling (below left).

Comfortable seating welcomes you into the cosy, top-lit den with its cork flooring and ethnic rugs (above).

The serene meditation room (right) is positioned in the calm at the top of the house.

CHAPTER 7

green building options

The ultimate in recycled building materials (above and opposite), forming Earthship walls from used car tyres, glass bottles, and cans.

Now we come to what Robert Laporte of Econest (see pp. 104–9) calls the "bones" of the house. What materials and construction methods will you use to build your house? Much will depend on what is most appropriate for the climate and location. Are there abundant natural materials on site – stone, wood, or earth (suitable for earth-building), for example, or any materials that can be reused or recycled? If not, what natural materials are most appropriate to your area and can be sourced locally?

If you are going to self-build, consider carefully which materials and building techniques you will be able to handle and enjoy. Research different materials, note pros and cons, look at local houses built using different techniques, assess costs and availability, and draw up a shortlist. If you are considering unusual materials, seek early advice from local planning and building control offices.

Conventional local materials, however, may not meet your eco- and healthy building criteria. Concrete, bricks, blocks, and stone, for example, are common building materials and, although strong and long-lasting, have what is called "high embodied energy". But, this also depends on how you source and specify them. To lessen the impact, use recycled aggregates in concrete,

and build with recycled bricks, blocks and stone. Or, if new, use them sparingly for where they are essential. In most of our featured houses, reinforced concrete was used for foundations, structural beams, and earthquake protection.

To meet eco- and healthy building criteria, a new wave of unconventional materials has emerged. It encompasses rediscovered older methods, such as straw bale and timber (from sustainable sources and without toxic treatments). It also includes new recycled-content materials, such as "Rastra". And it also embraces used consumer items, such as car tyres, cans, and bottles. Insulation materials are an interesting example of this. Newly developed natural options are cellulose (from recycled paper), sheepswool, flax, cotton, and woodfibre. Another new arrival on the eco-building scene is bamboo, that remarkable, fast-growing renewable material that is both lightweight and strong.

Natural building is much more than choosing "politically correct" materials. It is also about the spirit and timeless qualities of a material and the joyful and sensual experience of working with it. As Finnish architect Alvar Aalto, renowned for his simple use of natural materials, always advised: "allow the materials to express themselves."

Straw bale

Once you overcome your childhood associations with the Big Bad Wolf and an insubstantial "house of straw", you will be pleasantly surprised to learn that straw makes an ideal natural building material. Compressed into bales and stacked like giant bricks on each other, straw can be used to build sturdy and durable walls quickly. Straw is natural and nontoxic, and since it already is a waste agricultural product, has very low embodied energy. It is also cheap and abundant in many places. Moreover, it is a wonderful insulator from heat, cold, and outside noise. And, contrary to popular opinion, straw bales do not readily burn and are quite safe if their surface is sealed with plaster. But if a fire does start, they will smoulder slowly, thus allowing occupants time to escape. Water and fungal growth are the main enemies, but a "good hat and shoes" (a damp-proofed base raised well above ground level and a wide, overhanging roof) should keep the straw-bale walls dry. Flat roofs are possible, but may cause problems, particularly with rainwater drainage.

Straw-bale walls can be load-bearing (if locally approved) or non-load-bearing (the bales infilling or wrapping around a prebuilt structure). The first courses of bales are secured to metal rods in the stone or concrete footings. Subsequent courses are tied to those below with wooden pegs or metal rods, and sometimes with mortar. For load-bearing walls, a "wall plate" at the top is firmly strapped down to the foundation with reinforcing rods. The surface is then plastered with earth, lime, or cement stucco, with or without wire mesh. One advantage of non-load-bearing walls is that the structure, such as a timber-frame, can be erected and roofed over first, thereby providing shelter to store the bales and build the walls.

Orchard House (see pp. 120–5) was part-built with straw-bale walls (some were cob) within a timber-frame structure, while a variation of straw bale – a system known as "Baleblock" – was used for the curved, load-bearing walls of Spiral House (see pp. 90–5). Building with bales is easy to learn via the many courses and workshops,

and is ideal for the self-builder, with a little help from family and friends. As always, seek advice on the necessary planning approval, building regulations (codes). Yours may be the first straw-bale project in your area, and you may need to help and persuade officialdom.

Straw-clay

A much older method of construction is straw-clay or light-clay. This has been employed in buildings in Europe for centuries and is currently enjoying a revival. In Germany it is known as *leichtlehm* and was once common infill walling in oak-frame buildings – much as mud "wattle-and-daub" walls were used. Recently, to reduce weight and increase insulation values, experiments have included mixing clayey/sandy earths with lightweight aggregates, such as pumice, wood chips, expanded clay, and vermiculite, but straw-clay has become the most popular. This is partly due to the pioneering work of Econest-builder Robert Laporte, who has taught and built with straw-clay in both North America and Europe.

The Laporte technique uses a lightweight mix as infill between deep-dimension timber-frame members. In a process that is more akin to mixing bread dough than building, a fine clay slurry, or "slip", is combined with long stems of straw in a large trough or pit and left to sit for 12 hours before use. It is then compacted in a 30cm (12in) wide temporary "formwork", which is removed the same day to allow the wall to dry. Depending on climate and weather, this may take some time.

Once dry, the surface is plastered with an earthen-plaster or lime finish applied directly to the wall. This creates a handsome wall that is both strong and "breathable", and has a high thermal mass and insulation value. To increase insulation, more straw is added to the mix. Robert varies the mix to give more mass (more clayey-earth) to walls on the south side of the house and more insulation (more straw) to those on the north side. As straw-clay walls are non-load-bearing, permits or approvals are usually more forthcoming – but check first.

Cob

An earth-building method particularly suitable for lay builders is "cob". Wet mud is moulded by hand, again much like bread dough, into soft, hand-sized "loaves". While still plastic, these are stacked on top of each other to build up the wall. No formwork or special equipment is needed. Finally, when dry, the walls are finished with natural plasters. Although used for centuries in places such as Devon, England, cob had largely fallen into disuse, until it was revived by innovators such as Gernot Minke in Germany and by Ianto Evans and Linda Smiley, via The Cob Cottage Company, in North America. Their Oregon Cob method is aimed at helping people to build their own small, low-cost houses. Individuality is the key. The sculptural, free-flowing, organic designs with their arched windows and doors, plus their many endearing whimsical touches, make them perfect little natural homes. Orchard House was built mainly of straw bale, but parts were built of straw-clay and cob – the cob fireplace, for example, that the owners helped to create.

Earth is a versatile and expressive building medium, and there are many other methods you can explore. First, find out if your soil is the right type for your chosen technique. The most suitable types are sandy-clay or clayey-sand "mineral" subsoils, which are found beneath topsoils. These are ideal for techniques such as rammed earth or pisé (compacted earth walls) and adobe (sun-dried earth bricks), and compressed earth blocks (using brick-making machines). But for superadobe (earth bags), a wider range of subsoils can be used.

Abundant natural materials: an unfinished straw-clay wall at Econest (above left); a cob-and-thatch playhouse in Sweden (left); and straw-bale work in progress (opposite).

Sustainable wood

Wood is one of the most beautiful, useful, and satisfying building materials to use. The vast range of hardwoods and softwoods offers a plethora of colours, scents, grains, and textures. It even grows more lovely with age. Structurally, timber is good both in tension and compression and, with reasonable care, timber-frame or post-and-beam buildings will last for centuries. But although wood has been used for building from time immemorial, it is a dwindling and precious resource. If you are planning to build your house of wood, it is vital, from the ecological point of view, to insist that any new wood comes from sustainably managed forests. The Forest Stewardship Council (FSC) sets international standards and has established national systems to certify sustainable timber supplies and products.

Even better, try to find and reuse old timber in part or all of your house. Submerged "old-growth" timbers were rescued and reused in the Funk Homestead (see pp. 28–33), old, on-site wood was reused imaginatively in Green Condo (see pp. 76–81), and various "reclaims", including wood from a disused wine vat, now grace the interior of SunHawk (see pp. 134–9).

Healthy wood

When buying new wood, ask for untreated supplies. Treated wood may have been impregnated with toxic chemicals, such as the preservative pentachlorophenol and the pesticide lindane. Certified wood producers are encouraged to use least-toxic systems. Find out what has been used, but if you are still unhappy, choose from the range of safe, yet effective, alternative treatments, such as borate-based preservative and solvent-free products, that are on the market now. Some chemically sensitive people react to turpenes in aromatic woods, such as pine and cedar, but safe wood sealers can be considered. But free from harmful treatments, wood is one of the most delightful and healthy materials you could wish for. Warm to the touch, noise softening, and sometimes subtly scented, it is also a

regulator of indoor climate as it "breaths" and helps stabilize humidity and improve air quality.

Expressing the tree

If you live in a forested area, it is natural to want your house to be built of local wood. More than this, you will want the design to express its beauty, strength, and timelessness. And this is exactly what the designs of Posts Standing and Tree House do (see pp. 16–19 and 52–7). Opting for a solid post-and-beam structure, the architect specified huge de-barked logs to be the main posts – so striking that the house was named "Posts Standing". Whereas the light, springing timber design of Tree House is also aptly named, as it evokes the life and joy of a living tree. Both owners were fortunate to have forested land and, to compensate for the few trees that were used, the ability to replant new ones. Even if you do not have the land, you can still contribute to the many tree-planting projects around the world.

Timber framing

Another natural building success story is the revival of timber framing. Perfected over many generations by trial and error, it reached its peak in medieval times in forested countries of Northern Europe. Oak, being one of the most widespread and durable woods, was usually the preferred medium. Frames developed from simple "cruck" A-frames to more complex "box frames" with jettied or cantilevered upper storeys. The spaces between the frame members were interfilled, typically, with "wattle-and-daub" (interwoven hazel sticks covered with clay mixed with straw, cow hair, and dung) and finished with a coating of limewash.

Many of these medieval buildings survive today and are testimony to the good sense and craftskills of their builders and to the care and attention by their many owners down the years.

In North America timber barns were constructed in framed sections and erected at festive communal "barn raisings". Even though modern building techniques made these redundant, a love for old-style honest carpentry has survived and inspired a younger generation to revive and develop these venerable techniques. It is largely due to networks, such as the Timber Framers Guild of North America and their equivalents in Britain, that timber frames are becoming popular again. A good example is The Econest Building Company (see p. 106), where Robert and Paula have successfully combined sustainably sourced timber framing (with Japanese design influences) and baubiologie (healthy building) to create fine natural homes.

The Segal Method

In England, as the medieval timber-frame tradition gave way to brick- or stone-walled buildings, wood was mainly relegated to internal stud partitions, floors, and roofs. Except for some experiments with "stud-framed" houses ("stick frame"), and a few imported Scandinavian log houses, building whole houses from wood was rare. Recently, some housing developers have started to use stud frames again, but often only as the inner leaf of a cavity wall, the exterior wall being built of brick or rendered blockwork.

But well before this, in 1963, an architect called Walter Segal built a temporary timber house in his backyard. His aim was to perfect a method that could be accessible to all. Everyone should be able to build his or her own house. What he came up with was a modest post-and-beam structure that could be built quickly and cheaply using standard-sized materials bought off the shelf at any builders' supplier. Foundations were kept to a minimum. Since his death, advocates of this method have carried, incorporating eco- and healthy building criteria. Many low-cost homes have now been built using the Segal Method, from individual houses to large multi-unit communal projects. The design of Springfield Cohousing (see pp. 40–5) was inspired by the spirit of Segal's work, but uses different load-bearing construction techniques.

Old and new: a recycled timber roof and rustic tree post at Shenoa Retreat (above left), and new timber from managed sources at Tree House (above).

Prefabricated walling systems

Although "prefab" systems have been used for houses for many years, it is only recently that they have combined environmental and energy-saving criteria with their more well-known benefits such as factory-production and speed of construction. One such system is "Rastra".

Known as an "insulated concrete form" wall system, it is made of a lightweight material called thastyron (85 per cent recycled styrofoam – from such items as used plastic cups and fast-food containers– mixed with a cement binder). The waffle-grid form becomes a permanent framework once its reinforced cavities are filled on site with concrete. The system can be used for load-bearing walls, lintels, and retaining walls that, it is claimed, are strong enough to withstand hurricanes, tornados, and fire as well as termite and rodent attacks.

The material is not only lightweight and can be worked with woodworking tools, it has high sound- and energy-insulation values. Factory-produced prefabricated wall panels can be made to suit any building plan and are delivered, with reinforcement (ready to take on-site concrete), and with window and door frames intact. Walls can be straight or creatively curved, and this flexibility was used to great effect by the architect when designing SunHawk (see pp. 134–9).

Building with waste

While staying in an Earthship rental (see pp. 64–9), you will come across a sign in the kitchen asking you to please save all your boxes, glass bottles, and cans as they will help to build another Earthship. And, sure enough, when you visit one being built, there you will see crates of bottles and cans waiting to be used. Also heaped about the site are piles of old car tyres – another precious building material. When filled with compacted earth, they make rammed-earth "bricks" encased in the steel-belted rubber of the tyre. (Used cardboard lines the bottom to contain the earth.) The rear load-bearing walls are built up with these "bricks", laid in staggered patterns, and mortared strongly in position with cement. Non-load-bearing and internal walls are constructed with used aluminium cans, glass bottles, and cement. A special glass bottle cutter removes the necks so the wider bottom part of the bottles can be built into the wall. The cans and bottles are sometimes buried in the wall or exposed on the surface in decorative patterns. At the front, a long solar "greenhouse" constructed of timber frame and glass completes the shell.

Prefab or waste: "Rastra" prefabricated form wall system was used at SunHawk (opposite, far left); walls from recycled waste materials for Earthships (left, below, and above).

8 TESUQUE ECONEST

The promise of Econests is healthy living in buildings based on baubiologie principles – natural, nontoxic materials, solid frames of sustainably harvested timber providing the "bones" of the house, and straw-clay making the earth-skin walls. Underfloor radiant heating for comfort and deep eaves and rain chains protect the home from the elements.

The Casita guest house (above) adjoining the main house, linked by a covered breezeway.

A Japanese-style garden design including stepping stones, pond, and "rain chain" in the intervening courtyard (opposite).

Most people like to think of their homes as being "safe as houses". Pollution, it is often thought, is something that occurs outdoors and does not affect you once you are safe behind your own front door. Unfortunately, this is not the case. Indoor pollution and Sick Building Syndrome (see p. 25) now affect a growing number of people as more and more chemicals and other pollutants invade our homes as part of building materials, appliances, and cleaning products.

Architect Paula Baker-Laporte gradually realized that she was becoming chemically sensitive after reacting badly following building site visits during which she had been exposed to a host of chemical-laden materials. She traced the origins of her sensitivity to formaldehyde exposure during the time she lived in a new mobile home. Although this situation could have become serious enough to bring her career to an end, it was her study of "baubiologie" – an holistic, healthy building discipline that originated in Germany (see p. 26) – that prevented this happening.

With new perspectives in mind, Paula learned of the work of healthy homebuilder Robert Laporte. Originally a timber-framer from Canada, he was another baubiologie enthusiast and teacher, and well known for his wide knowledge of natural building methods and materials. When Paula saw that he was running a workshop in Colorado, she jumped at the chance to take part. Thus started a collaboration that has led to a rewarding partnership, both personally as well as professionally. Ever since, when Robert is asked how to build a natural home, he always advises "first, find yourself a good architect!"

Their opening project was to find somewhere to build their home. Robert had seen what, at first sight, looked an unpromising hillside location above the village of Tesuque, New Mexico. But, its reasonable price, proximity to Santa Fe, and wonderful mountain views persuaded him that this was the place.

Although the site's main problem was erosion caused by unimpeded storm water washing down the hill, its natural shelter and southerly

The living room in the Tesuque Residence, looking through into the dining area (above). Natural daylight is provided via rice-paper ceiling panels and back-up heating is provided by a fine masonry stove.

aspect would make it ideal, once major remedial work had been done. Moving poorly sited pinion pines and resculpting the landscape with terraces buttressed with "gabions" (rock-filled cages) stabilized the land and absorbed the water. Since then, the couple have transformed the area with their first home, Paula's office, Robert's workshop, and a couple more homes – or Econests, as they call them – designed and built by their Econest Building Company.

It was a real pleasure to meet up with Robert and Paula again and be able to stay a short while in their 37 sq m (400 sq ft) Casita – guesthouse – adjoining their new 176 sq m (1,900 sq ft) Tesuque Residence, their latest Econest. It was

late September and there was a spell of unsettled rainy weather with dramatic thunder and lighting. At the 2,135m (7,000ft) altitude, it was getting chilly, especially at night, yet inside the Casita it was always warm and comfortable. Having removed our shoes, Japanese-style, the pale bamboo floor felt pleasantly warm with its radiant underfloor heating. The single large space, with en-suite bathroom, extended out into two window bays or recesses – one for a Mexican-type built-in bed and the other for a long reading table with drawers. The exposed peg-jointed timber frame was handsome. The smooth earth-plaster walls had gently rounded corners and, if you looked carefully, you could see little specks of mica

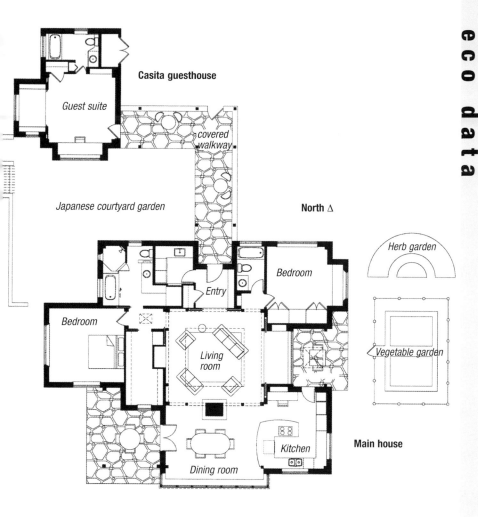

Casita guesthouse

Guest suite

covered walkway

Japanese courtyard garden

North △

Bedroom

Entry

Herb garden

Bedroom

Living room

Vegetable garden

Kitchen

Main house

Dining room

e c o d a t a

CONSTRUCTION
• Timber frame with light straw-clay "breathing" walls
• Metal roofing

MATERIALS
• Nontoxic, healthy materials
• Sustainable bamboo flooring
• Earthen floors and wall plasters
• Sustainably harvested local white fir
• Slate kitchen counters

SOFT ENERGY SYSTEM
• Wind-powered electricity purchased from the State
• Extensive use of daylight so no electric lighting needed during the day

HEATING
• High insulation levels
• Passive solar gain retained in adobe walls and floors
• Back-up Tulikivi wood-burning stove
• Radiant floor heating powered by gas-fired water heater (rarely needed)

COOLING
• Wide roof overhangs shade summer sun
• Natural ventilation
• Roof vent system
• No mechanical cooling required

WATER
• Rainwater harvesting and storage in cisterns for landscape irrigation

LANDSCAPE
• Major site restoration with tree moving/planting
• Organic gardens

shining in the plaster. The windows looked out onto a formal Japanese courtyard with pond, boulders, and stepping stones. To reach the main house, you wandered around the courtyard under a covered "breezeway".

Designed with Paula's fine attention to detail, the buildings combine the best of Robert's timber-framing techniques, baubiologie principles, and carefully chosen natural and healthy materials. The solid frames constructed of sustainably harvested local white fir are the "bones" of the house, as Robert describes them; the 30cm (12in) thick leichtlehm, or straw-clay (see p. 98), infill walls are the "flesh"; while the earthen wall plasters are the "skin". To reduce rotation or twisting, Robert works the wood green and designs special timber joints to limit movement. The straw-clay walls are built up off low, stone-faced concrete walls and are protected from rain by 1.2m (4ft) roof overhangs. The walls are finished with earth plasters; ochre-tinted with yellow iron oxide for the living spaces, and green-tinted with copper carbonate for bathrooms. They are "breathing" walls, allowing a gradual transfer of air and moisture between inside and outside without loss of energy efficiency. This, combined with the mass and porous nature of the materials, moderates indoor temperatures and humidity to create comfortable and stable conditions. A well-windowed south-facing "sun bump", as Robert calls it, gives plenty of solar gain. On really cold days, radiant floor heating affords extra warmth plus, if needed, at soapstone Tulikivi woodstove.

Rainwater from the roof is channelled into massive underground cisterns for irrigating the restored terraced landscape and Paula's organic garden, where she grows most of the herbs and vegetables they need. The salads and home-grown pumpkin soup were delicious! All kitchen compost goes to further improve the garden's soil.

Japanese influences (with touches of Arts and Crafts and Frank Lloyd Wright) are subtly felt everywhere in the house, from the shoji screens and tatami mats of the meditation area to the rice-paper skylight in the living room. The shallow-pitch and gabled rooflines, with their generous overhangs and corner "rain chains", strongly evoke the traditional houses and temples of Japan.

The solid timber and earth structure, refined and understated design, natural muted tones and hues, subdued lighting, pleasant scent, and devoted craft skills all serve to create an atmosphere of serenity, peace, and calm. "Everything nourishes everything," comments Robert. To which Paula adds: "The house just "sings", it is built to last for many generations."

This view (left) shows a yoga and meditation alcove with Japanese shoji sliding screens, tatami mats, and a recess with focal object.

The outside dining area (below) enjoys beautiful mountain views. The projecting roof is supported, Japanese-style, by a timber post standing on a large, river-worn boulder.

Sunlight pours into the dining area from the terrace doors (opposite).

CHAPTER 8

choosing interior materials
walls, windows, and doors

A nautilus shell motif in stained glass (above) glows from the window at Spiral House.

A handcrafted entrance door at SunHawk faces east, toward the rising sun (opposite). The stained-glass panel is iridescent as it catches the light.

Even if you have not taken the whole journey and built your own natural house from scratch, it is very likely that you will be directly involved in the finishing and decorating of its interior. This is the principal area for do-it-yourself activity and the one where you can exert more control over what you use and how you use it.

When choosing the right natural materials for the interior, remember the "3 Rs" (see p. 22) to ensure their ecological pedigree, and give them a thorough health check to satisfy yourself that they are not toxic or harmful. Think twice before opting to buy new materials and instead look for recycled and reclaimed items first. If you are redecorating your existing house, use this as an opportunity to declutter your rooms and spring-clean your house. There is a lot of truth in the saying that "less is more". After you finish decorating, only reinstate what you really like – recycle the rest.

Healthy home issues are even more important when you come to the interior. Be careful to use only nontoxic materials. Avoid any materials (such as paints or adhesives) that contain volatile organic compounds (VOCs) as they "off-gas" (emit chemical vapours) over months or even longer periods. And avoid materials containing formaldehyde, too, as they will also off-gas and smell unpleasant.

Most modern soft furnishings – carpets, fabrics, upholstery, and bedding – contain artificial chemicals, and their combined effect is very injurious to healthy indoor air quality, especially in a home that is inadequately ventilated. Since we spend something in the region of 80 per cent of our time indoors, the materials we use in the interior will have a considerable effect on our health and wellbeing.

It is far preferable to accept only natural ecological and healthy materials. They have a "living" quality all of their own; they look good, feel good, and smell good (if they have any smell at all). If they are properly used, natural materials are generally safe. They are certainly extremely satisfying to use.

The good news is that many more alternative products are now available and they are becoming much more competitive in price. Even if they are still a little more expensive, it is worth spending the money to enjoy better quality, safer products that help you and help the planet, too.

Paints, washes, and stains

Most conventional paints are derived from petrochemical sources. Their ingredients and manufacture are harmful to your personal health and the environment. Worse, many of the synthetic solvents used are classified as carcinogenic or toxic. "Painters' dementia" (or solvent dementia) is a recognized industrial disease and can result in headaches, dermatitis, bronchitis, asthma, and illness of the nervous system. The WHO (World Health Organization) has found that professional painters face a 40 per cent increased chance of cancer. Around 90 per cent of our indoor environments are now covered with synthetic petrochemical coverings known to contribute to "Sick Building Syndrome". Most plastic paint seals in moisture and hastens rot and decay. So, avoid using these harmful products and switch to natural and healthy "breathing" alternatives.

Natural alternatives

Natural paints and stains have been specially developed to avoid the problems of petrochemical plastic products and be healthy for the user and benign in terms of the environment. Ingredients such as plant oils and resins, casein, waxes, plant-based solvents, and earth and mineral pigments are naturally occurring. They are, renewable and biodegradable and most plant ingredients are organic. Water-based formulae, instead of toxic VOCs, for emulsion, gloss paints, stains, and varnishes means they are harmless

Used for centuries, lime washes (above and below) declined with the introduction of modern emulsion paints, but fortunately they are now re-emerging. Used as plain white or tinted, they are suitable for exteriors and interiors of historic or modern buildings. Lime paints are healthy as they have natural, mildly antiseptic qualities and help walls to "breathe", readily allowing moisture to evaporate, thus deterring mould growth. Suitable for absorbent surfaces, such as stone, brick, plaster, and wood, they come ready mixed in a range of attractive washes.

and odourless, or have a pleasant subtle aroma, during application and drying. Microporous and hygroscopic qualities allow underlying materials to "breathe" and regulate moisture, humidity, condensation, and rot, and make for a better indoor environment. If you cannot source these alternatives, look for "low-odour" water-based products that have a very low VOC content. And as we know from our own experience, good decorating is three-quarters preparation.

Do you need to paint?

First, assess if you need to decorate at all. Even if you use ecological products, you are still using resources and indirectly contributing to pollution via their manufacture and transport, particularly if imported. New or recycled natural materials, such as brick, stone, wood, and plaster, often look attractive as they are and need little or no additional decoration. Similarly, wood needs only beeswax or natural wood oil to protect it and enhance the beauty of its grain. Wall plasters have many attractive surface finishes and natural in-built colours. If the paintwork is in reasonable condition, a wash down with a nontoxic ecological multisurface cleaner will remove dirt and grime and restore its original freshness.

Rethink paint stripping

Even though stripped wood looks great, getting there is messy, dusty, and hazardous. Paint usually contains toxic chemicals; even lead in the older layers. Most conventional paint strippers are, in themselves, toxic, emitting high levels of VOCs and should be avoided. If you use a hot-air gun (or blowtorch) take care or you will singe the underlying surface, burn yourself, or perhaps even cause a fire! Still want to go ahead? If so, send removable items, such as doors, away to a professional paint stripper. Use solvent-free, water-based alternative products (see pp. 152–5). Strip moveable items outdoors, and ensure maximum ventilation if working indoors. Always wear protective clothing, gloves, a facemask, and eye protection.

Water-based washes and wax glazes allow you to apply see-through tints on top of an emulsion base. This produces a translucent effect that is more vibrant and lively than opaque paint finishes. You can create special effects by applying overlays of different tinted washes or glazes, one on top of the other, and by using techniques such as rolling, stippling, and dragging. When dry, the wax-glazed surface can be lightly polished to a silk finish that is dirt- and water-repellant.

Shown here is the stairwell of The Steiner Centre, Baker Street, London

Some natural paint ingredients:

Linseed oil
Produced by pressing the oil from the seeds of the flax plant, usually boiled to improve drying times. Used as the binder in linoleum and many paint and varnish products. Strong, durable, and flexible.

Lime
Used for centuries in traditional wall paints, renders, and mortar. Product of heated limestone – the forerunner of modern cement.

Turpentine
Natural solvent for paint. Distilled from pine and other resinous trees. A renewable and biodegradable source, turpentine is a far better alternative to petrochemical solvents, such as white spirit, which contain toluene and xylene – both known carcinogens.

d-limonene
A natural solvent derived from citrus fruits, such as oranges, lemons, and grapefruit, which gives paints a wonderfully subtle fragrance. Produced by distilling the oil extracted after pressing the fruit peel.

Chalk
Natural calcium carbonate, used in various wall paints and lime renders as an extender and filler.

Natural earth and mineral pigments
These are used to colour paints, lime washes, and some renders. Pigments are simply extracted, cleaned, and milled. Some mineral pigments, such as ultramarine blue, are heat-treated to produce different colours.

If you would like to produce your own tints, natural earth and mineral powdered pigments are the ideal way. Use them in casein or emulsion, washes, or glazes, or even mix them directly into plaster. Before adding it to your chosen medium, simply soak the pigment overnight in some water. But if you want to mix pigments, do this when they are dry. You can also obtain pigments as pastes or concentrates.

Plasters and earth

Natural plasters have a long vernacular tradition in many cultures and, although they nearly died out in the Western world as cement and gypsum took over, they are gaining in popularity again.

They can be used internally or externally; the latter being termed "render", "stucco", or sometimes "pargetting". Their main function is to protect walls made of materials such as straw-bale, straw-clay, cob, and limestone from the elements, but they offer many decorative possibilities, too. Earth, lime-sand, lime-clay, and clay-dung are some of the main traditional types, but, as you will find out if you delve into this fascinating area, there are numerous local and personal variations. You can experiment by adding pigments, pumice, vermiculite, broken shells (such as mother-of-pearl), flecks of mica, or finely chopped fibres to the plaster mix. Or, as the Japanese used to do, blow iron dust evenly over the surface of a moist, white-plastered wall and watch it oxidize to give a warm brownish yellow tint to the whole. For extra protection, use beeswax or a "breathable" natural seal on unpainted plaster surfaces.

Vernacular use of natural plasters on traditional African huts in Great Zimbabwe (right and opposite). Indigenous styles use a range of earth pigments to decorate the walls.

Earth plasters

Using earth plaster is one of the pleasures of natural building. Maybe it takes us back to our childhood, when we played about with mud and water and got filthy. Unless you are a potter or sculptor, it is not likely that you will handle wet clay very often, but become an earth-plasterer and this delight is yours once more.

Mixing up clay with chopped straw, fine sand, and depending on the job, perhaps flour paste, milk, a little vegetable oil, or glue/size is a bit like mixing the ingredients for a huge cake. Earth plasters are applied as one or several coats varying in mix, consistency, and thickness, and spread over the wall using your bare hands and trowels. Finally, a thin coating of "clay slip" – containing flour, clay, kaolin, mica, fine straw, and maybe pigment – is brushed on to seal and beautify the surface.

If you do try your hand at these techniques, always do a test patch first to check that your recipe and application method work. And never use cement render on materials such as straw-bale, straw-clay, cob, and limestone, as the render will prevent the surface from breathing, trap moisture, and lead to decay.

Lime

"The older the lime, the better" is what traditional builders would say. To make "lime putty", as it is called, from scratch, add quicklime to water in a trough. (Never do it the other way round or it might explode.) This process is called "slaking", and as great heat and splashes of lime are produced, wear protective clothing. Rake the mixture and sieve it to remove any unburned bits. Then, store it for at least three months before use. Do not expose it to the air or it will not bind with sand when you come to make lime render or stucco. Traditionally, lime putty was stored in a pit, where it would rest for months or years; it was even passed down the generations.

Outside render uses coarser sand than inside plaster. It usually takes two coats, mixed with animal hair, chopped straw, or hemp to render a wall, and it is important to keep the coats moist and protected from the elements while they slowly dry. Lime plaster can be applied as a top coat to mud plaster or direct on surfaces such as straw-bale. Although simpler and safer, off-the-shelf bagged "hydrated lime" does not make such good lime putty. It is better to try and get ready-made mature lime putty from a supplier. For extra protection or decoration, coat with white or tinted limewash or, for a beautiful mottled-rust effect, apply ferrous sulphate while still damp.

Clay finish

Lying somewhere between a paint and a plaster, clay finish is a ready-made product that provides an attractive and unusual internal decorative surface. The rough-textured finish and subtle natural tints of this product are quite unique, and it has the advantage that both the final texture and colour are applied in a single time-saving operation.

Clay finish is produced in white and four basic colours, and they can be blended to give a very broad palette, offering you plenty of scope for creative application and stunning interiors.

Tiles

If you have natural plaster walls, there will be places where you need to protect them from fire, water, and the kicks and knocks of everyday life. Kitchens, bathrooms, showers, door and fireplace surrounds, hallways, and staircases are some of the wall areas where tiles can usefully help.

Apart from their utility, tiles offer a wonderful world of their own when it comes to style, shape, size, pattern, and colour. Before looking at new tiles, check if you can source reclaimed ones from an old building or architectural salvage company. Handmade tiles are particularly fine, but can be expensive. Wall tiles are one of the items in a natural home where it really pays off to buy the best. It is better to have a smaller area of beautiful tiles rather than a larger area of cheaper, mediocre ones. If you live near an area known for its tile-making, incorporate the local vernacular style into your home.

Hand-formed terrazzo bath-tub with mosaic-covered walls at Spiral House (right); clay floor tiles and a blue Mexican-tile border in a bathroom countertop at SunHawk (above right); structural exposure at Tree House (opposite); and a rustic wooden stair handrail from Orchard House (detail, opposite).

Mosaic

Using small pieces of brick, stone, pebbles, tile, glass, shells, or any other fairly hard material, you lay out your desired design or pattern and fix it in position using an additive-free grout. The Greeks and Romans used *tesserae* (small cut-stone cubes) and were expert at this mosaic technique, as witnessed by the many that remain to this day. But you do not have to use this method. The great thing about mosaic is that you can use up bits of waste material, such as smashed plates or broken tiles. Famous examples include the Watts Towers in Los Angeles and the celebrated "organic" buildings by Gaudi in Spain. Taken to new heights, the stunning free-flowing mosaic designs of James and Drew Hubbell are an integral part of most of their designs and sometimes cover whole walls and floors.

Before choosing tiles, check which adhesives and grouts can be used. Some contain harmful VOCs and additives, so try to choose tiles that work with nontoxic and additive-free alternatives.

Structural exposure

In some of the houses featured in this book the timber structure was also an integral and visible part of the interior walls. Tree House (see pp. 52–7) displayed "exposed structural craftsmanship" of timber that the owners desired (and built). The structural white fir frame of Econest (see pp. 104–9) serves as a natural interior framework into which earthen plastered walls and rice-paper screens seem to fit so naturally. In Posts Standing (see pp. 14–19), the massive log posts and vertical boarding create a stunning interior all by themselves. While in others, such as Funk Homestead (see pp. 28–33), you are conscious of the love of wood in the way it has been crafted with care everywhere around the house. Earthship, Green Condo, and SunHawk (see pp. 64–9, 76–81, and 134–9) demonstrate that recycled woods are important to use and offer special opportunities for design ingenuity.

Wood care

To protect wood, avoid chemical, solvent-based sealers, varnishes (polyurethane, for example), stains, and waxes, and choose from the wide range of alternative natural products that are available, such as plant and resin oils, and beeswax. These will care for your wooden interiors in a healthy and eco-friendly way, and will add their pleasant aromas to your home.

Cork

This tree product is made from the outer bark of the cork oak (*Quercus suber*) of southern Europe. Compressed bark strips and granules are made into sheets and tiles suitable for interior walls and floors. This natural and sustainable material – if properly harvested – possesses good thermal and noise-insulating properties, and it is also hardwearing and rot-resistant. Sheets and tiles can be supplied treated with surface varnishes or untreated, allowing you to use nontoxic finishes of your choice. Cork makes a good interior wall finish, giving a warm, rich-textured, noise-softening surface.

Wooden interiors

When we think of wooden interiors, pictures come to mind of solid, cosy log cabins, elegant oak-panelled interiors, or beautifully crafted redwood houses of the west coast of North America. They are surely some of the most comfortable and pleasing interiors of any natural home. If you are contemplating using wood, bear in mind the general advice on sustainability (see p. 100). And, remember to ensure your designs meet fire regulations (codes), and choose wood that is either naturally resistant to pest attack or treatable with nontoxic applications (see pp. 152–5). Look for architectural salvage, too, as it is not unheard of for whole wooden interiors to be dismantled from old buildings and reassembled in new ones. Maybe there is a walnut-veneered Art Deco room, complete with geometric clock and light fittings, waiting for you – if you can afford it! Or, if not to your taste, look for some oak-panelled bays that you could use to line a wall or two – these will certainly be more affordable.

Windows

As the "eyes" of the house, windows play an important part in the design of your natural home. Think about the function you want each window to fulfil. One of the main jobs in a solar home is to ensure that the windows on the sun-facing sides of the house are orientated and designed for passive solar gain. This does not mean that whole walls have to be windows, for overglazing will lead to overheating. You will need most on the south side and less on the east and west, and a few small windows on the north for light and ventilation. But their exact deployment depends on where you live.

Design on a 12-month basis to take account of the sun's changing seasonal path. In summer the sun will have a high, arching path and a lower one in winter. At midday in winter, the sun's low rays will penetrate deep into your home and bring warmth, while at noon in summer the almost vertical rays will only reach a short way in. To avoid overheating, have wide roof overhangs and window shading devices on all south-facing windows. Shade west-facing windows from afternoon summer sun as well.

Adequate daylighting is vital for health and energy saving. To maximize daylight, have tall windows and roof lights that let in a lot of sky. To improve the quality of interior daylight, have light coming from more than one direction.

Light-admitting recycled glass bottles inset into an Earthship wall (below); the bathroom moon window at Funk Homestead (bottom right); and the oval window seen through the double barn entrance doors at Orchard House (right).

Orientate your windows to encompass an attractive or interesting view, if you have one. But if you do not, at least have a small, judiciously placed window to frame a particular feature – a lovely tree, for example, the western sunset, the eastern dawn, or summer and winter solstice windows, as at SunHawk.

Unusually designed and beautifully shaped windows add a sensual dimension to an interior, as does the ovoid-shaped window at Orchard House – the organic window seat there being the perfect companion.

A wide choice of energy-saving windows is available. Look for those fitted with "low-emissivity" (low-e) glass as double or triple panes. Avoid using uPVC plastic-coated frames, especially in older-style houses, as they usually destroy the original design with their thick, bland edges that do not match the originals.

Doors

How you make an entrance into your home is important. It is the first impression people have of your home and hopefully it will be a positive one. It is not just a matter of having a front door – you are creating a welcoming experience. Japanese homes like to have "intermediate spaces" between outdoors and indoors. These act as transitions between public and private spaces – a verandah being an example. Another example is the *genkan*, or formal entranceway. Here, shoes are removed before you enter the house. To delineate the entranceway, there is a slightly raised floor level and, traditionally, a stone step. Flowers, incense, and a carefully prepared view of the garden all add to the feeling of hospitality as you enter the house. Both Econest and Orchard House have well-designed entrances, and each unit in Springfield Cohousing has its own entrance porch. Echoing another tradition,

that of the Native American lodge, SunHawk and the Hut Earthship have front entrances that face east, to the rising sun. Spiral House has its large portico entrance facing the sunrise, too.

Once you have created the context, you can concentrate on the entrance door. Rather than buy a standard door, look for something interesting in a reclaimer's yard or consider having one made. A number of the feature homes incorporate stained-glass in their doors – Spiral House has a lovely iris flower design found in a flea market.

With recycling in mind, Green Condo has eye-catching entrance gates made of reclaimed Volvo hatchback doors. Actually, Michael Kauffman did buy interior standard doors for Spiral House. But when he had "distressed" them they looked old and in keeping with the pueblo feeling of the house. And to get away from rectangular doors, try arched and pointed shapes, or experiment with a "moon door", as at Posts Standing.

The entrance porch and feature doorway at Spiral House (top); and the reclaimed Volvo hatchback doors that form the very individual entrance gateway to Green Condo (above).

9 ORCHARD HOUSE

Built of earth, clay, and straw, this house is built in an old orchard and its design is inspired by the local farm barns, with their wide doors and high ceilings. The result is an exciting open-plan space with a curving south-facing solar façade allowing for interior greenery. The orchard also accommodates a smaller, straw-bale guesthouse.

Although there are many apple orchards around Occidental, California, lower prices of imported fruit have made the local produce less competitive. As a result, some growers have had to sell up. When one of these orchards came on the market, teachers Patsy Young and Annie Scully, from nearby Santa Rosa, decided it was too good an opportunity to miss and acquired the 2 hectare (5 acre) plot.

They could see where their house should be sited – it called out to them! They knew it was to be a modest house and as ecological as it could be. And they were certain that it had to be built of natural materials because of the feelings they evoke of warmth, solidity, and harmony with the planet. Annie knew about straw-bale construction, having lived at the Shenoa Learning Center in Philo, where the first code-approved straw-bale house had been built some years previously. Patsy was not so sure and, at first, did not take to the straw-bale building she saw. This soon passed, however, as she became familiar with the material.

The next step was to visit the Real Goods Solar Living Center in Hopland (also built with straw-bale), to ask about a builder. They were referred to Tim Owen-Kennedy and his cooperative natural building company, Vital Systems. Tim, in turn, recommended Darrel DeBoer as architect to help Annie and Patsy create their house plans.

At their first meeting on site, Darrel quickly came up with some sketches that expressed the owners' ideas and their 111 sq m (1,200 sq ft) house soon began to take shape.

Taking inspiration from the local farm barns, Darrel produced an open-plan design with high ceilings and wide entrance doors. The spacious main living space – now known as "the big room" – with its gently curving glass wall and heavy floor, is ideal for passive solar gain. It is a lovely and graceful space, too. Leading off this is the kitchen/diner, sunroom, and laundry/storage with second bathroom. On the first floor is a study and bathroom featuring a large half-moon window and straw-bale seat, and up again is the top-floor sleeping loft.

Darrel and Tim worked as a team from the start and the traditional boundaries between architect and builder fast disappeared as they developed the house from concept to detailed plans. Tim often worked out details using clay models, while Darrel would pitch in with the hands-on building work. Darrel firmly believes that any architect worth his salt should be able to build what he designs. This partnership allowed the building to develop naturally and to introduce the element of surprise as one of the duo interpreted the other's ideas in an unexpected and, usually, pleasing way. It is, as they admit, a design-on-site process that has to take into account the non-standard nature of natural and

These two views show the sun-facing façade (above and opposite) as well as the upper level, which houses a bathroom, small office area, and bed loft.

salvaged materials. When plans went in for approval, they were met with a little scepticism, partly due to straw-bale still being a relatively new concept, and partly due to the plans being rather less detailed than the county expected. The latter, however, was intentional, to allow for developments in the construction process. But

good relationships were established and, in the end, Darrel was invited to help rewrite the county straw-bale codes.

The structure of the house is anchored by the two-storey, timber-frame tower at the rear, from which runs a ring beam around the edge of the house supported on rustic wooden posts. The timber-frame walls are infilled with straw-bale, pinned together with bamboo. Straw-clay (leichtlehm), and/or cob is used for internal partitions and sculpting the fireplace. The walls are then finished with earthen and lime plasters. The living room floor, also earthen, proved more

The dramatic barn doors open wide to give a view of the "big room" (below). Japanese influences can be seen in the inclusion of a rustic post, stepping stones, and large ceramic water jar.

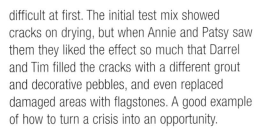

Inside the "big room" (top) showing the oval window and rustic upper-level balcony. The same window can also be seen here (above left).

The stove sculpted into a cob-and-boulder fireplace (above).

difficult at first. The initial test mix showed cracks on drying, but when Annie and Patsy saw them they liked the effect so much that Darrel and Tim filled the cracks with a different grout and decorative pebbles, and even replaced damaged areas with flagstones. A good example of how to turn a crisis into an opportunity.

It is also an example of how Tim's crew acted as artists as well as builders. There were many instances where they brought their own creative spirit and individuality to the project. Such an example was Evan, the carpenter, who designed and built the oval-shaped window and cob bench seat in the "big room", which adds so much to the space. The crew was always on the look-out for salvaged materials, too, and a storm-wrecked barn offered all the old redwood they needed.

All the earth used was dug from the site and the material from the large hole in front of the house became the floor — the hole is now due to be landscaped as a pond. Other items remain for completion when further finance is available, such as the kitchen and bed loft, but as Annie and Patsy found — the real fun is in the making of the house. They are very satisfied with their natural home and every time they return they say how blessed they are to be there.

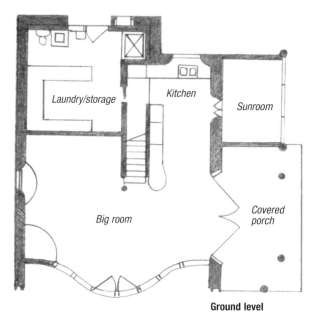

Laundry/storage

Kitchen

Sunroom

Big room

Covered porch

Ground level

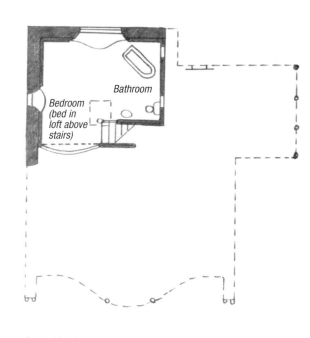

Bathroom

Bedroom (bed in loft above stairs)

Second level   North △

eco data for orchard house

CONSTRUCTION
• Timber frame infilled with straw-bale pinned with bamboo (considered by the building department to be a standard wood-frame structure even though it used less lumber than conventional construction)
• Internal partitions of leichtlehm (straw-clay for sound insulation) or cob
• Earth and lime-plaster finishes plus limewash outside
• Clay paints inside
• Earthen ground floor
• Recycled metal roofing

MATERIALS
• Reclaimed madrone wood floors
• Renewable rye grass board ceiling
• Salvaged redwood and applewood trim and madrone posts
• Materials-efficient front door and sunroom doors of laminated honeycomb (same construction as industrial "clean rooms")

ENERGY SYSTEM
• Photovoltaic system was installed remotely, ground-mounted – it was considered easier there due to the curvature of the roof

HEATING
• Wet-blown cellulose roof insulation
• Heavily insulated north walls (to prevent heat loss) and west walls (to prevent heat gain)
• Passive solar gain and heavy mass ground floor
• Metal box fireplace built into cob/stone chimney piece
• Rarely used radiant tubing in the mass floor

COOLING
• Reflective roof covering
• Super-insulation to prevent heat gain
• Wide roof overhangs to shade summer sun
• High ceilings and tower windows to vent warm air
• Wide external doors to help "flush" interior
• Open mezzanine floor to help convection

WATER
• Solar water heating system plumbing in place – panels can be set when funds become available
• Well

LANDSCAPE
• Pond to be completed soon
• Orchard apple trees retained around house
• Drought-tolerant planting

Exterior view of the curving solar windows and wide roof overhang (right).

Inside the Gatehouse living room (below right), looking toward the open-plan kitchen.

Gatehouse

Since the Orchard House was built, Darrel has finished another small guesthouse near by. Called Gatehouse, it is a curving, single-storey structure with solar windows taking up most of the sun-facing façade. The rear is a well-insulated straw wall with small windows high up to assist in the natural ventilation.

Inside, the gently curving space contains an open-plan living room with compact kitchen at one end, and a bedroom with en-suite bathroom at the other. Darrel is an advocate of the benefits of bamboo and is experimenting elsewhere with designing and building innovative, strong yet lightweight, structures. Here, at Gatehouse, he has planted a bamboo variety called moso – the same type used to make flooring in China – along the north entrance wall. When fully grown, moso will reach a height of 19m (60ft) or more and it serves as extra weather protection and produces a cooling air movement around the building. In summer, the air inside a bamboo grove can be 8°C (15°F) cooler than adjacent areas

Between building Orchard House and this one, Darrel realized how much straw-bale construction is a labour sink. There are so many opportunities for customizing that the commonly held belief "it must be cheaper" is rarely true. So the effort here was to make straw-bale construction more into a system that could rival the several-hundred-year headstart that light wood framing has.

By using strong, 5 x 15cm (2 x 6in) box posts and beams and thin plywood, a great deal of wood was saved, and the structural elements were light, easily handled, and well insulated. And by making the covering structure essentially a shed roof, it went together simply.

Between the box posts, a wire mesh was installed on the inside and outside of the walls to provide the structure with great strength, enabling the whole building to work as a single unit – when one point is under stress, the load is distributed to hundreds of nearby nails and ties.

By spacing the joists further apart than usual more material was saved, and each joist sits on top of a post, eliminating the need for headers. The wood needed for this building was about a third that required for conventional, light-gauge framing, yet the performance in terms of heat loss and wind/earthquake resistance is anticipated to be dramatically better than average.

choosing interior materials
floors

Reconditioned timber floor from Green Condo, phase one (opposite and above), with debarked timber columns featuring.

Like shoes, floors are visually very important. They are often treated as being only functional, but, since they occupy such a large area of any room, they strongly influence its visual impact, ambience, and the general impression of comfort. Floors can be used as a free-flowing design element, especially in open-plan layouts, where their surfaces (and perhaps levels) change as they "move" from place to place. Laid as a design element, not just as a material, they delineate spaces and give visual and tactile clues to how they are to be used. Floor surfaces are often one of the last jobs to be finished, but what a difference they make!

Taking your shoes off before entering the home (as many people do in Japan and Scandinavia) shows respect for the house. Walking about in bare feet, socks, or soft slippers not only keeps floors clean, but it is quieter, more relaxing, and saves on wear and tear. Slightly uneven floors are more relaxing to walk about on, too. Traditional earth and plaster floors can have this quality and, where safe to do so, are worth experimenting with.

But you do need to be practical, too, and choose a natural material that is right for the space and also meets your ecological and health criteria. These range from stone, brick, and tile for hard surfaces, through wood, earth, cork, and linoleum for medium wear, to natural fibres (seagrass, coir, sisal, and rushes), rugs, and carpets for softer surfaces.

To meet sustainability criteria, first choose reclaimed or recycled flooring. Used wooden floorboards and parquet blocks can be found, as can used floor tiles, flagstones, slate, and brick paviers. But they might cost more than you think. Otherwise, look for renewable materials from sustainable sources and products with eco-labels (see pp. 152–5).

To have healthy flooring, avoid plastic flooring such as those containing PVC, and check out wood laminates to see what they are made of and how they have to be fitted. Avoid toxic floor adhesives, stains, paints, and varnishes. Many factory wood-floor systems can be fitted together as a "floating floor" without any adhesive. For those who are allergic to dust, dust mites, and chemicals it is best to keep it simple and choose a hard, inert surface with a few rugs laid on top that are easily cleaned.

And, when thinking of comfort and warmth underfoot, consider underfloor heating, either via a hot air "hypocaust" or piped hot water system.

Exposing original floors

An old floor of wood, brick, stone, or tile can be a beautiful asset to any home as long as it is made of good materials and is structurally sound. Before you decide to cover it with something new, assess if it is worth restoring – a less resource-hungry option. It may have been patched and repaired over the years with ill-matching materials; if so, you may be able to cannibalize replacements for these from elsewhere in the house, or hunt for them locally in reclaimers' yards or building waste dumps. Some old floors, especially wooden ones, may have settled and not now be perfectly level, but this is all part of their charm. So, if they are not too bad, or likely to be unsafe, resist the urge to rectify this. Unless done very carefully, levelling a timber floor can cause a lot of needless damage to the old floorboards as they are taken up to allow wedge-shaped "firring pieces" to be fixed underneath. Renovating floors to their former glory may take a lot of work and could be

prohibitively expensive if done professionally. However, it is an ideal job for a do-it-yourselfer, since most of the work, although painstaking, is relatively straightforward. For a wood floor, removing old coverings, extracting endless tacks and nails, and cutting out and replacing boards takes a lot of time, patience, and care. If you decide to sand the surface, take precautions (see p. 129). Treat the surface with natural, nontoxic oils, stains, varnishes, and waxes. The original timber floors in Phase 1 of Green Condo were restained and seamlessly matched and repaired.

Concrete floors

If you have an old, damp-proofed concrete floor that is in good condition, you could try grinding off the top surface to expose the aggregate beneath. Depending on the original aggregate used, this can give an interesting visual effect, similar to terrazzo, when finished with polish, wax, or varnish.

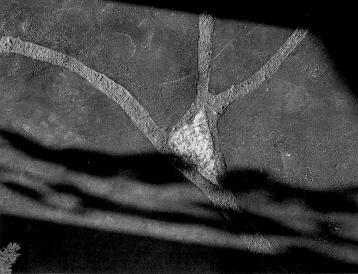

The exposed and polished original floor at Green Condo (top); the poured-earth floor at Orchard House with cracks filled with tinted grout and pebbles as a design feature – making a virtue of a mistake (above); and bamboo flooring and tatami mats used at Tesuque Econest (opposite).

Wood flooring

Traditional wood floors usually consist of solid wooden floorboards nailed to timber floor joists that span between the walls of the house. This is known as a "suspended floor". For greater rigidity, and to avoid gaps, tongue-and-groove boards are used. To prevent rot and warping, timber floors are best used only where conditions are dry and well ventilated – for these reasons, upper floors are preferred. Wood floors are not usually recommended for bottom floors unless they are raised well above the ground, or where the subfloor beneath (usually concrete) is free of damp and there is adequate ventilation between the subfloor and the timber floor above.

If you are the owner of solid wood floors, take care of them, and rather than smothering them with wall-to-wall carpeting, let the beauty of the grain be seen and admired. Every board was part of a growing tree and it is a great waste to

bury them beneath inferior coverings. If you sand the surface of the old boards, you should use a "dustless" sander and wear protection for your nose, mouth, and eyes. Finish the job with natural sealers, oils, or waxes.

If you are installing a solid wood floor, look for recycled wood first, but if you are using new wood always insist on it coming from sustainable sources. Avoid endangered tropical hardwoods and seek locally grown alternatives. Since solid wood floors are fairly expensive and use up a lot of trees, cheaper, factory-made wood flooring systems are being marketed.

Because these are floor finishes – not structural – they have to be laid over an existing floor or subfloor. Sometimes called "laminate flooring", the thin tongue-and-groove boards have either real wood (or a plastic wood effect) veneer bonded to plywood or another base. They come with a factory-cured finish, such as urethane, or unfinished for you to seal, wax, or varnish as you choose, and they can be fitted as a floating floor or fixed to the subfloor.

Before deciding on using one of these systems, find out what the boards (and the surface veneers, underlays, and adhesives, if needed) are made of and if they contain any toxic or unpleasant chemicals.

Bamboo flooring

One of the fastest-growing and most readily renewable resources is bamboo and it is gaining in popularity as an alternative to wood flooring. Sold as tongue-and-groove, three-ply boards or panels, they are available in a flat or vertical grain and in a light-blonde colour or a darker brown. They come unfinished or factory-cured with urethane or similar. Some makes specify sustainable sources and non-use of pesticides and fertilizers. Bamboo makes a tough, yet attractive floor and is well worth considering.

Earth floors

Another way to lessen the impact on the world's forests is to avoid having wooden floors and use earth instead. Mention installing an earth floor to most people and the suggestion will meet with derision. However, despite this a well-laid earth floor is a joy to live with. It is resistant to wear, stains, and scratches, quiet to walk on, easy to clean, and needs little in the way of maintenance. But best of all, earth floors look lovely with their subtle variations of clays, and their smooth solidity feels comforting.

Being solid and heavy, they have good thermal mass and are ideal for passive solar buildings (to store the heat of the sun and release it slowly to warm the house later). When building an earth floor, for extra comfort, and warm feet, consider installing underfloor heating via a piped hot water system – preferably a solar-heated one.

Earth floors have to "breathe" and so do not have a vapour barrier underneath. Instead, they use a thick base layer of gravel or crushed rock to prevent rising damp. Insulation may not be necessary either as long as the perimeter walls and foundations have some. But if you do want to include this, use a granular type, such as vermiculite, perlite, or expanded clay.

Poured earth floors are still the vernacular in some parts of India, Asia, South America, and the southwest of the United States. They are built up in two or three layers of finer and finer material until the floor is 7.5–20cm (3–8in) thick, depending on the room size and use. Since each layer dries very slowly, plan ahead and pour them only in dry, warm weather. Wait for each to dry properly before adding the next. When the whole floor is thoroughly dry, finish with boiled (not raw) linseed oil and beeswax – the more coats used, the harder wearing the floor will be. Cob Cottage Company and Econest Building Company have both developed earthen-floor techniques.

But earthen floors are not ideal where there will be a lot of water or heavy use. Better for these conditions are harder, impermeable materials, such as flagstones, brick, slate, or tiles.

Green Condo's (recycled-aggregate) concrete floors had dyed and varnished surfaces. The opportunity of scoring patterns in the wet cement resulted in floor art, such as the "anniversary window" design (see below). Orchard House turned a problem into a virtue when the earthen floor mix (stabilized with a little cement) cracked. Using flagstones to replace the worst-affected areas, pouring tinted grout into the cracks, and decorating them with tiny pebbles and bits of shell and glass transformed the whole floor into a piece of organic design!

A poured concrete floor at Green Condo, phase two (below), with tinted panels to mark the shifting path of the sun on co-architect, Cate Leger's, birthday; the recycled glass terrazzo counter top at Green Condo (opposite, above); the mosaic snake motif at the entrance to Spiral House (opposite, below).

Floor tiles and mosaic

Although the materials that tiles are made of are generally healthy and nontoxic, the accessories that go with them may not be. Tile backings, such as particleboard (chipboard), may contain formaldehyde, and sealants, adhesives, mortars, and grouts can contain other harmful chemicals, additives, and fungicides. Backing boards are needed in timber stud houses, where tiles cannot be fixed to a solid surface, such as brick or block wall. Using the wrong tile backing in wet places or areas of high humidity will lead to mould and rot. Look for formaldehyde-free boards and, for wet areas, use a water-resistant building board. And instead of using ready-mix mortar, mix your own so you know what it contains. (See pp. 152–5 for suppliers of other nontoxic materials.)

Floor mosaics

Floor mosaics are laid in a similar way to wall mosaics (see p. 116), and they are also traditionally made of small cubes of stone, glass, tile, and pebbles. They are very labour intensive and unless you are prepared to lay out the design yourself, a mosaic will be expensive to produce. But if you use recycled waste materials, such as broken tiles, you can have fun making your own effects.

Terrazzo floors

Another traditional floor technique is called terrazzo. With this, small pieces of marble (or even ground, recycled glass) are mixed with tinted cement. The mix is then poured and spread out on the floor in sections delineated by brass strips. When it is dry, the surface and brass divisions are ground smooth and polished to give a rich, shiny surface.

Being hard, easy to clean, and water-resistant, terrazzo is ideal for other uses: kitchen counter tops in Green Condo and Spiral House, for example. In Spiral House, terrazzo was also used for a bath tub. It is a versatile, yet affordable technique and with different aggregates and tints can suit many situations and styles.

Carpets, rugs and natural fibres

Think twice before buying new carpeting for your home. Although it is associated with comfort and luxury, most modern carpet, like conventional paint, is a complex mix of petrochemical-based synthetics that are not good for the environment or for your health. Tests have shown that there can be more than a hundred chemicals in one carpet, many of which are known to be neuro-toxins. Emissions from carpets may include xylene, styrene, formaldehyde, toluene, and 4PC (4-phenyl-cyclo-hexene). Health problems associated with off-gassing chemicals can range from headaches, breathing difficulties, asthma, and general anxiety and depression to reproductive disorders, neurological malfunctions, and even cancers. And it is not just the carpet itself, it is also the toxic chemical gases emitted from the backing, underlay, adhesives, and carpet cleaners that can compound the problem.

Healthy carpet

One strategy is to avoid completely having any carpet in your home. The thinking here is that with all the chemicals that a carpet might contain, it is impossible for the average consumer to evaluate if it is safe to buy or not.

The next strategy is to look for labels that claim the carpet is "hypoallergenic" or approved by a carpet industry scheme, such as "Green Tag" in the United States. But can you trust these?

Or you can decide to consider carpets only made of natural materials, such as seagrass, coir, sisal, cotton and wool, with felt underlay. This should be a safer and surer option, but if you find 100 per cent natural-fibre products, ask if they have been treated – pesticides are used extensively on cotton, so choose organic cotton. Seagrass and other "natural carpeting fibres" may have a synthetic latex backing containing off-gassing chemicals. So choose products that need no backing, and use a natural (not synthetic) felt underlay. All-wool carpet may have been treated with toxic mothproofing pesticides. So choose untreated wool. And when fitting the

carpet, have it grip-fitted or tacked and avoid any adhesive or sticky carpet tape. And rather than wall-to-wall carpet (harbouring dust, dirt, and allergens), buy better-quality natural wool or fibre rugs that can be moved around and cleaned more easily. Finally, initiate a shoes-off policy.

The middle way

But if you do decide on a conventional synthetic carpet, go down the least-harmful route. Ask for manufacturer information and avoid any products with factory treatments, such as fungicides or stain-resisters. Take a sample home and do a smell test and avoid any that have an unpleasant aroma. Unroll the carpet and let it air in a well-ventilated place for as long as possible before fitting. Avoid synthetic foam backing or underlay, and use felt, and avoid adhesives.

Sheet flooring, floor paints, and dyes

PVC plastic flooring has become so widespread in kitchens, bathrooms, and utility areas because it has many advantages. It is durable, cheap, easy to clean, and water- and stain-resistant. But vinyl chloride is a carcinogen and flooring can off-gas, especially when new. Also, there may be problems with mould in humid areas. Therefore, it is not acceptable in a natural home.

Cork

As with walls (page 117), cork makes a fine flooring finish. Sold in tiles or sheets, it is a flexible, quiet, warm, and yielding floor surface, as Michael Kauffman found when he laid it in his home office in Spiral House. Unsealed, it may have a slight aroma, which, again, most people find pleasant. But if you prefer a scent-free floor, seal it with a natural, nontoxic sealer.

Natural carpet covers the stairs at Green Condo (opposite), while the den at Spiral House (right) uses warm, and quiet, cork as a floor covering.

Natural linoleum

Linoleum has all the advantages and none of the disadvantages of PVC flooring, except that it will cost a little more. Natural linoleum is made from renewable ingredients: powdered cork, linseed oil, wood resin, and wood flour mixed with chalk, and pressed on to a hessian (burlap) backing or jute canvas. Be sure to buy the natural product rather than a synthetic version. Strong and flexible, natural linoleum comes in a wide range of colours (some particularly vibrant), and can be used creatively to make almost any floor pattern you like. It has, for most people, a pleasant and healthy aroma, so do not spoil it by using a toxic adhesive to fix it down. Use a wood lignin paste or safe, benign product (see pp. 152–5).

Floor paints, stains, and varnishes

Traditionally, preserving wooden floors involved staining, oiling, or waxing them. This not only helped to deter woodworm and other destructive pests, it also protected the surfaces against damp and mildew. It made them more durable and easier to clean and over the years they would take on a beautiful deep glossy patina, like that of an old antique. Medieval houses have some of the loveliest wooden floors you can imagine. Rather than trying to replicate this effect using petrochemical stains and polyurethane varnish, use healthy and renewable floor finishes (see pp. 152–5). Also, choose nontoxic floor paints and sealers for other flooring materials you wish to cover.

10 SUNHAWK

The concept of this house is based on the roundhouse of the indigenous Pomo people, and inspired by the celebration of the solar cycle. Autonomous living with state-of-the-art eco-technology and permaculture principles makes this home a demonstration of the best in sustainable design and a place to be shared as a learning experience.

I f any couple should know how to create a sustainable home it is John Schaeffer and his wife Nancy. John founded Real Goods in 1978, the first ever solar retail business, now located in Hopland, Northern California, and the Solar Living Institute, an environmental education nonprofit organization. Nancy, who has lived off the grid since 1973, joined Real Goods in 1989. So, using their combined 43 years of experience in renewable energy, they embarked on planning their dream homestead.

They knew they wanted a home that would be far more than a shelter. It needed not only to promote sustainability and be energy-independent, nontoxic, and gentle on the environment, but also it had to be stunningly beautiful, soothe the soul, and nourish the spirit. But beyond it being a home for themselves, they also hoped to have space for Solar Living Institute classes, gatherings, and educational permaculture.

Their previous experience of permaculture creation at the 5 hectare (12 acre) Solar Living Center had taught them that finding the right site and planning the landscape around a house is just as important as the design of the house itself. After much searching, John and Nancy found a "raw nugget of paradise" just a short distance up a dirt road from Real Goods with breathtaking views of the surrounding valley and Duncan Peak. It was totally off-grid – no developed water, no electricity, no sewage system, primitive roads, and no phone lines. They even had to build a bridge over a creek to access the property.

The first project was to dig a 2 hectare x 80cm (5 acre x 2ft) deep pond both for recreation during the hot summer months and to provide passive cooling for the house. Fortunately, the soil was mostly clay, very conducive to pond building, so no liner was necessary. At one end, to celebrate the natural springs, they added a secret grotto, waterfall, and clover lawn. Then they created a lush permaculture landscape of Spanish grasses, a coastal redwood grove, lavender, yarrow, and local tree varieties. Now this attracts all manner of wildlife, from herons and snowy egrets to bull frogs and ducks.

The south-facing façade (above) showing the eyrie with solstice and equinox viewing points.

The stained-glass image of the hawk (right) that symbolizes "vision" to Native Americans – sun streaming through the window makes the hawk "fly" across the floor to join up with a matching hawk symbol.

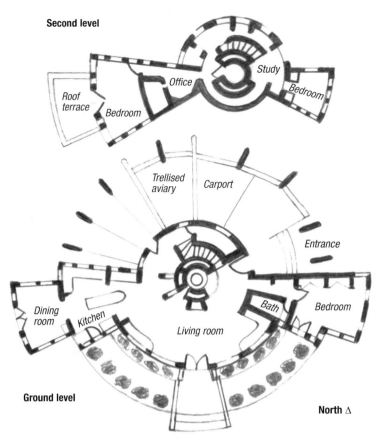

Second level

Roof terrace

Bedroom

Office

Study

Bedroom

Trellised aviary

Carport

Entrance

Dining room

Kitchen

Living room

Bath

Bedroom

Ground level

North △

The central open-plan living space (opposite) showing the radial roof structure, upper walkway, focal soapstone stove, the tree of life, and the SunHawk image in the foreground.

But where was the best place for the house? As there was no hurry, they spent time camping out on likely sites, finally settling for one that Nancy had originally liked best. On a slight rise, it overlooked the pond and offered full southern exposure – ideal for passive solar design and for the proposed vegetable garden and the fruit and olive orchards. They next started to search for an architect to share their vision, and were fortunate to find Craig Henritzy.

Craig suggested a house concept based on the California Native American roundhouse of the indigenous Pomo Indians. Oriented exactly to the cardinal points, and patterned after a red-tailed hawk, the house was named SunHawk. Craig's initial plans for a 418 sq m (4,500 sq ft) house were too costly and, with their three children away at college, too large. So the plan was reduced to 270 sq m (2,900 sq ft) for the three-bedroomed, one-and-a-half-bathroom home.

After numerous revisions, the final circular plan revolves around a central "fountain room"

painted with a mural of their land and local wildlife. A spacious living space has curved bench seating running around the perimeter to provide extra seating for Institute classes, and the room has a woodstove as focal point. Leading off this in one direction is the open-plan kitchen/dining room (John and Nancy's pond wildlife lookout), and in the other a kid's bedroom and bathroom. A gracefully curving Mexican-tiled staircase takes you up to a circular walkway (overlooking the living room below) and then on to John's office, bathroom, and master bedroom, with its roof terrace and stunning views. Further up a spiral staircase you arrive at an eyrie at the top of a tower called "the eye of the hawk", which has fresh breezes and a 360° vista.

John and Nancy soon found that the project was taking up almost all of their free time. So, in order to cope, they decided to live on-site while building work was going on. As temporary accommodation, they built a simple storage barn and installed 15kW of used photovoltaic modules. This is still there and, with more modules and storage batteries, provides solar electricity for the house and all the couple's outdoor electrical needs, including extensive water pumping. During the rainy season, this is supplemented by a 1.5kW hydroelectric system driven by the water of the seasonal creek.

To meet their goal of sustainability, Nancy spent countless hours researching materials and appliances. The roof finish was an example of this research. Having looked at everything from copper to composition shingles, she found rubber shingles made entirely from recycled car tyres that looked exactly like slate from a distance. She also sourced as many salvaged materials as possible – for example, the wood from a disused wine vat was ideal for cupboard doors, as was the wood from a dead walnut tree for the kitchen worktops.

In 2001, their chosen master builder, Steve Gresham, broke ground. Mindful of the risk of earthquakes in the area, Steve convinced them that deep concreted footings were absolutely

eco data

CONSTRUCTION
- Rastra block walls
- Foundation: 115 cubic metres (150 cubic yards) of reinforced 6-stack concrete/fly ash mix

MATERIALS
- Recycled redwood (roof decking, fascia, and some barge rafters) recovered from winery, Soledad, California
- New redwood from sustainably harvested sources
- Recycled Douglas fir timbers reclaimed from a naval warehouse, Bayone, New Jersey
- Walnut floor reclaimed from walnut orchard, Chico, California
- Walnut cabinets and counters reclaimed from dead tree at Solar Living Center

SOFT ENERGY SYSTEM
- 17kW photovoltaic panels (4kW Astropower 110w modules, 13kW Siemens 75w modules recycled from former Real Goods project)
- Harris hydroelectric turbine producing 1.5kWh
- Plus trace inverters, combiner boxes, and batteries (158kWh storage)

HEATING
- Passive solar, super-low-emissivity windows, massive thermal mass
- Radiant heat floor slab powered by solar hot water panels
- Back-up Tulikivi soapstone woodstove

COOLING
- Earth tube system – rock storage under cooling tower with two 46m (150ft) culverts. Cool air drawn up with two solar pumps and convected to the rest of house
- Evaporative cooling from 12 hectare x 80cm (5 acre x 2ft) deep pond

WATER
- Deep well pumped by Grundfos solar water pumps
- Solar hot water system

LANDSCAPE
- Permaculture garden, orchard, and pond

essential. The main load-bearing structure was Rastra – a strong, lightweight, and highly efficient insulating material made from 85 per cent recycled styrofoam beads and 15 per cent cement. This was finished on the exterior with stucco and on the interior with plaster. Large, sun-facing windows allow for passive solar gain, while heavy-mass concrete floors store the heat to warm the interior. Active heating is via solar-heated water as radiant underfloor heating, backed-up (if needed) with a Tulikivi high-efficiency soap-stone woodstove.

To keep the house cool, even in the hottest months, a unique design was used. In the middle of the house, a small "cooling room" was built over a deep rock bed sunk 2.75m (9ft) in the ground with two culverts extending 46m (150ft) further down. Two solar-powered fans draw cool underground air – always an ambient 67°F (19°C) – up into the room to cool the entire house.

Solar symbolism is an integral feature of the house. A stained-glass hawk above the south-facing garden doors "flies" across the living room from west to east when lit by the sun. On the winter solstice, at noon, the projected image of the hawk aligns exactly with a slate hawk set into the floor in front of the woodstove.

The whole process of designing and building SunHawk has been "one of the most rewarding experiences of our lives" say John and Nancy. "We hope to spend the rest of our lives here, free from fossil fuels, the electric grid, telephone wires, and highway noise. As we walk lightly on the Earth we have attempted to set a positive example that anyone interested in solar living and permaculture can learn from. And, of course, we are thankful to have a comfortable home surrounded by nature to enjoy with each other and share with our children and grandchildren."

One of the Mexican-tiled staircases (right) that winds upward around the central core of the house.

personal style and decoration

The cool breezeway linking Tesuque Econest with the Casita guesthouse (opposite) uses a calming design and natural materials.

Whether you are creating a new or renovated natural home, or just remodelling a room, you will want interior furnishings and appliances that complement and express your ecological lifestyle. But most mass-produced furniture suffers from the same problems as modern building materials. What looks like wood, is actually a thin veneer of wood or wood-effect plastic glued to a chipboard (particleboard), medium-density fibreboard (MDF), or plywood base. The baseboards and glue may contain formaldehyde. If solid wood is used, then it is probably coated with a petrochemical finish. Cushions will be filled with plastic foam or latex and the furnishing fabrics may be synthetic, too.

So when buying new furnishings, remember the wider environmental and ethical picture. Are the materials from renewable and sustainably managed sources? Is there a record of exploitation of workers, especially if the material is imported from the developing world? Are "fair-trade" and ethical practices used? What are the environmental policies of the company? In fact, just as if you were buying an antique, you want to know its provenance: here, its "environmental provenance".

But how can the average consumer find out about all this? Look for "green" and health-status labelling (see pp. 152–5), but better than this, start researching well before you need to make the purchase and ask environmental, ethical trade, and consumer organizations for advice on acceptable suppliers.

Otherwise, let your personal inclinations be your guide to style and taste. The planet could not care less if you choose traditional or modern, country-style or urban chic as long as you avoid damaging her in the process! And your home definitely does not have to evoke an atmosphere of "lentils and sandals".

If anything, it will probably show indicators of your green and healthy preferences and tendencies. There will be an emphasis on more individual and unique furnishings, rather than mass-market products. A mix of older recycled and reclaimed items will co-exist happily alongside new sustainable acquisitions. There will be a preponderance of locally produced items over those imported or transported long distances. And hopefully, like the Japanese concept of *shibui* (creative restraint), the spaces will display a few beautiful and cherished natural items rather than a clutter of the mediocre. Not only will the natural spaces evoke a feeling of inspiration, not aspiration, they will be places of harmony with the earth and peace for body and spirit.

Living spaces

The living spaces in the houses featured in this book all demonstrate, in different and imaginative ways, how to combine passive solar living with comfort and style. Orientation to the sun's path and solar symbolism are skilfully intertwined in SunHawk's semi-circular, open-plan living space, with its many sun-facing windows, flying shadows, and solar alignment of the "sunhawk" motifs. At the Funk Homestead, the sunken kiva-like living space, with its polygonal timber roof, served as the core of the house and the meeting place of the east and west wings. The "big room" at Orchard House, with its gently curving solar window bay, did indeed have the feeling of a high-ceilinged barn, which was its inspiration. The serenity and calm of the Econest living room, blended Japanese influences with practical passive solar design via the dining area "sun bump". Tree House's double-storey windows soaked up the sun and looked out onto fabulous views. Posts Standing evoked native traditions of the Northwest with its massive log posts, but set in a contemporary context. Spiral House showed how the pueblo style of the Southwest could be ingeniously adapted to make a gracious, curved living space that was ideal to retain the warmth of the sun. Green Condo and Springfield Cohousing both had compact, sun-facing living areas, yet their open-plan living/kitchen/dining arrangements made them feel spacious.

In many, the focus was the fireplace, but care had been taken to install energy-efficient stoves – such as the wood stove in Orchard House, hand-built brick masonry stove in Posts Standing, and Tulikivi soapstone stove in Econest and SunHawk. Each used thermal mass to retain and slowly release the heat. The open fireplace in Spiral House was used occasionally as back-up during cold winter snaps.

Solid wood furniture was much in evidence, some being heirloom pieces, some rustic, some modern, some hand-me-downs, and some just simple, recycled pieces, such as shelf units and kitchen tables. Ethnic items, often collected locally, brought exotic touches to some homes and were especially fine in the meditation room at the top of Spiral House.

The kiva-style central living space at Funk Homestead (opposite); the dining space linking the living area with the "greenhouse" at Hut Earthship (left).

Electromagnetic radiation

Controversy still reigns over the possible hazards of exposure to low-level electromagnetic radiation in the home caused by the plethora of electrical wiring and equipment. Cases of child leukemia have been reported, especially where the bed has been placed close to an incoming main. To be on the safe side, take precautions and sleep as far away as possible from electric cables, sockets, and "live" items, such as lamps, clocks, radios, and televisions. Switch off and unplug these while asleep or use battery-operated models.

Sleeping spaces

We spend about a third of our lives asleep. Where and how we sleep has a fundamental effect on our waking lives. Sleep well and you are much more likely to live well. You will stay healthier and cope better with the stresses and strains of everyday life. Sleep badly and your whole life will begin to suffer. Being constantly tired and irritable makes you function poorly and may lead to ill health. Since we spend so much time asleep, where and on what we sleep assumes great significance.

The space To help you sleep well you need a peaceful room. Choose one that is away from traffic and other sources of noise, or if this is not possible, noise-proof the windows and doors. If feasible, choose a room that receives morning sun. Then, do everything you can to make the space tranquil and relaxing by, for example, using soothing colours and soft lighting.

Keep the space as simple and free of clutter as possible – clothes, books, ornaments, television, and other electrical goods. Feng shui has much to say about bedroom layout and the best position for the bed. There is also the theory that to sleep well you need to align yourself north–south in the direction of the Earth's magnetic field. The bedroom is also a private and personal space; a place to take refuge, seek rejuvenation, and make love. Owing to a shortage of space, it often has to double as a retreat or sanctuary for the practice of meditation and healing therapies, such as yoga or massage. Hence, another reason to keep the decor simple and uncluttered.

Sleeping spaces: the magical, circular bedroom in Hut Earthship (opposite, above); a restful sitting bay in the master bedroom at Funk Homestead (opposite, below); and a hand-made quilt in the master bedroom at Tree House (above).

The bed Once you have created the right atmosphere for rest and sleep, concentrate on having the right bed. Old beds may be too soft and not give enough support, while new ones may be too hard.

A lot depends on individual weight, anatomy, and personal preferences and trial and error may be the only way to find what is best for you. With a soft bed, try putting some boards under the mattress to make it firmer. With a hard bed, put a softer covering, such as a futon, tufted-wool under-blanket, or "organic" cotton-filled mattress pads, on top of the mattress. Better, though, is to invest in the best-quality bed and bedding you can afford, but make sure they are made of non-toxic materials and finishes, and natural fibres and fabrics. Treat yourself to 100 per cent pure "organic" cotton bed linen (see pp. 152–5).

Recovered timber features as the counter top in a phase two kitchen of the Green Condo project (left); a phase one kitchen can also be seen (below).

Cooking and dining spaces

"The heart of the home" is how the kitchen is generally regarded and this was borne out in our featured homes. In Spiral House, the focal point from which the spiral design for the whole house sprang was the curiously shaped island counter top in the middle of the kitchen. In most houses, the kitchen and dining spaces were not separate, but sociable extensions of the open-plan living space. The owners of SunHawk admitted that their kitchen/dining space was one of their most used spaces, more even than the sitting area.

The kitchen is the gateway to your productive garden and the outside market. It is the place where food arrives and recycling begins. SunHawk and Econest both produced home-grown food and had "intermediate" spaces between garden and kitchen – verandahs and lobbies – to allow for muddy boots and vegetable cleaning.

Like modern furniture, new kitchen cupboards and cabinets present another minefield for the would-be natural homer. Whereas the doors and drawer fronts may be solid wood, these usually have solvent-based finishes. Inside, the carcasses (cases) are often built of melamine-covered chipboard (particleboard) containing urea-formaldehyde binders. To overcome this, ask for

units made with formaldehyde-free boards (see pp. 152–5) or solid wood, although this will be more expensive. To offset the extra expense, rethink the layout of your new kitchen and settle for fewer cabinets. Like roads, the more cupboards there are, the more they fill up. Alternatively, reject modern kitchen units and revamp old kitchen dressers, solid-wood cupboards, and recycled tables. And when designing the layout, consult the cook! In addition, do as your grandmothers did, and have a cool larder or pantry for extra food storage. Whatever you decide, have separate recycling receptacles for cans, glass/plastic bottles,

paper, card, and plastic waste. And compost all of your organic kitchen waste.

Many modern kitchens are full of resource-hungry gadgets that flatter energy-consuming lifestyles. If you cannot do without them, then go the next best route and use the best-rated energy-saving appliances you can find. Look for energy-efficient refrigerators, dishwashers, washing machines, and dryers and use low-energy lighting (see pp. 152–5).

In certain areas, using natural gas for cooking is a greener option than electricity. If you do use gas (including bottled gas), have your appliances checked regularly to see they are working safely and efficiently. Combustion gases are some of the worst offenders for causing indoor pollution. And be aware – carbon monoxide kills. Have adequate ventilation to extract unpleasant cooking smells, moisture, and any harmful or toxic fumes.

The kitchen at Spiral House (top), with its unusual terrazzo counter top; the open plan kitchen/dining area at Orchard Gatehouse (above).

Bathrooms (left to right): Green Condo, Econest Casita, Green Condo, Hut Earthship.

Bathing spaces

In today's natural bathrooms, bathing goes far beyond hygiene – it has become a therapeutic and nurturing experience for body and soul. The rejuvenating and sensual pleasures of water and its healing power, known to many ancient cultures, have been rediscovered. As more people sample the delights of outdoor bathing in spas, thermal baths, and hot tubs, the concept of bathing and nature have been reunited. This has influenced the way bathrooms are designed, making them less closeted and more open to the outside. At Funk Homestead, a large moon window beside the bathtub gave tranquil views of the wooded slopes and forest outside, while in Orchard House a large semicircular straw-bale bathroom window gives an unrestricted view of the orchard below. Even if you are overlooked, you can still create this impression using an obscured-glass window, or bay, filled with indoor plants.

Water seems to bring out the creative spirit. In SunHawk, the upstairs bathroom was fringed with Mexican tiles and the downstairs shower room was aglow with mosaic and ceramics. In Spiral House, the bathtub was cleverly free-formed in vibrant terrazzo. In Econest, tinted mica-flecked earth plaster, stone tiles, and glass blocks gave a subtle and elegant effect. While in Earthship, recycling was uppermost with the flagstone and tinted cement tub, and recycled bottle wall decoration.

Bathrooms are another area of the house ideal for equipping with salvaged items. But only accept fixtures and fittings in good condition and avoid any that are chipped or stained or cannot reasonably be brought up to modern plumbing standards. You can have great fun searching for the style you want to create – Victorian, 1930s' porcelain and chrome, or luxury hotel – but remember that old toilets are water guzzlers, so

if they cannot be refitted with a modern interior it may be better to buy a new low-volume-flush model. The salvage route may prove to be more expensive, but you will end up with a unique and individual design that will be a real joy.

Otherwise, bathrooms are all about water and how to use it pleasurably, yet wisely. Fittings have undergone a water-saving revolution and you can choose from devices such as tap (faucet) flow restrictors and water aerators, low-flow shower-heads, and low-volume and dual-flush toilets (see pp. 152–5). Installing a water-recycling system allows greywater to be used to flush the toilet or irrigate the garden. Or, consider water-free options

such as waterless urinals and composting toilets. Designs of these have now been perfected to give smell-free, low-maintenance service.

If possible, install a solar water-heating system to provide hot water for the bathroom and space heating for the home. Or install a "condensing" boiler (tankless/on-demand water heater). Going further, consider a heat-exchanger to reuse heat from bathroom greywater elsewhere in the home.

To complete your natural bathroom, choose "organic" cotton towels, a washable natural-fibre shower curtain, and nontoxic personal cleansers and bathroom cleaners (see pp. 152–5). Always keep the bathroom clean and well ventilated.

Nature spaces

As concern grows about unhealthy, mass-market processed food, more people are turning to "organic" and fresh, locally grown produce. The best way to achieve this is to grow your own.

John and Nancy had a thriving permaculture garden at SunHawk, and Paula grew delicious "organic" vegetables at Econest. Even in the heart of downtown Berkeley, some of the residents of Green Condo used their balconies to grow herbs and tomatoes.

And at Springfield Cohousing, plans were afoot for a communal vegetable garden to join the free-range chickens. If you are not able to enjoy home-grown food, look for fresh, local produce in organic and wholefood stores, at the growing number of farmers' markets, or join an organic "box" home-delivery scheme.

Solar windows, sunspaces, and conservatories are ideal places for plants and, in colder climates, they offer an equitable, year-round growing environment. Here, you can cultivate flowers, fruit, vegetables, salads, and herbs. You can also experiment with exotic tropical varieties, such as bananas, that grew so happily in Earthship's "greenhouse". Properly maintained indoor planting also helps to regulate humidity within the home and improve indoor air quality.

Conserving water outdoors is as important as it is indoors. The key to this is to plant species

that are suitable to your local soil and climate conditions. They will be naturally hardier and more resistant to local circumstances and will need less maintenance as a result. Plant drought-resisting plants in hot, arid areas (as at Green Condo), and cover the soil with a thick layer of mulch, bark chippings, or pebbles to retain the moisture. Irrigate in the cool of the evening to lessen evaporation and use rainwater stored in butts, or larger storage tanks, or greywater from the bathroom and kitchen. When planting, dig in the compost you have made to improve the fertility of the soil.

In all climates, help to conserve groundwater by directing rainwater not down the drain, but back into the soil as many of the homes featured in this book did, such as Springfield's rills, pond, and swale, and Econest's rain chains.

Wildlife protection and minimal environmental impact on the locality should be fundamental to the design of any natural home. Ideally, these

The permaculture garden at SunHawk (opposite), with its new foot pond behind; the garden at Permaculture Institute, Point Reyes (above), viewed from a cob garden shelter; the meditative, Japanese-style courtyard garden that links Tesuque Econest to the Casita (top right).

need to be taken into account from day one when you buy your plot, or move into an existing home. Keep a record of the flora and fauna in the garden and ask locally what visitors to expect. Seek advice from local wildlife organizations on how to attract a greater variety of species (and how to deter unwanted ones).

Ponds are great attractors of wildlife, and birds and butterflies respond quickly to the creation of the right habitats. Using organic or permaculture gardening techniques will also boost natural wildlife. At Tree House, "wildlife corridors" will allow undisturbed passage of local species. SunHawk's "foot pond" and sensitive landscaping had already been blessed with the arrival of new wildlife. And at Funk Homestead, except for the organic garden and orchard, the rest of the land had been retained as permanent natural habitat, allowing local deer to migrate on their ancient trails.

RESOURCES

Architects of featured houses

Posts Standing
Henry Yorke Mann
www.henryyorkemann.com

Funk Homestead
Jeff Gold & Associates
www.jeffgoldassociates.com

Springfield Cohousing
Architype Ltd
www.architype.co.uk
www.users.waitrose.com/~cohouses

Tree House
Sage Architecture, Inc.
www.sagearchitecture.com

Hut Earthship
Earthship Biotecture
www.earthship.com

Green Condo
Leger Wanaselja Architecture
http://lwarc.com

Spiral House
Birkani Architects
Birkani@aol.com

Tesuque Econest
Baker-Laporte & Associates, Inc.
www.bakerlaporte.com

Orchard House
DeBoer Architects
www.DeBoerArchitects.com

SunHawk
Craig Henritzy
Henritzy@mindspring.com

Chapter 1
Design for natural living

Gaia
www.ecolo.org/lovelock
www.gaianet.fsbusiness.co.uk
www.gaiabooks.co.uk

The Carbon Trust
www.thecarbontrust.co.uk

Building Lifecycle Carbon Calculator
www.cyberium.co.uk/carboncalculator/

The 3 Rs
Waste Watch
www.wastewatch.org.uk

DTI
www.dti.gov.uk

Green Street
www.greenstreet.org.uk

Energy Saving Trust
www.est.org.uk

Save Energy
www.saveenergy.co.uk

Recycling
www.recycle.mcmail.com

Rethink Rubbish
www.rethinkrubbish.com

Recycle More
www.recycle-more.co.uk

Institute for Local Self-Reliance (ILSR)
www.ilsr.org

Embodied energy/lifecycle analysis
http://cig.bre.co.uk/envprofiles

Reclaimed materials
Salvo
www.salvo.co.uk

Healthy houses
www.healthy-house.co.uk
www.hhinst.com

Formaldehyde information
Environmental Protection Agency (EPA)
www.epa.gov/iaq/formalde.html.

EMFs
Environmental Protection Agency (EPA)
www.epa.gov

Healthy Home Center
www.healthyhome.com

Less EMF
www.lessemf.com

Human Radiation Effects
www.electric-fields.bris.ac.uk

MCS
American Academy of Family Physicians
www.aafp.org

Sick building syndrome/health hazards
London Hazard Centre
www.lhc.org.uk

Baubiologie
International Institute for Bau-Biologie & Ecology (IBE)
www.buildingbiology.net

Breathing walls
Excel Industries
www.warmcell.com

Feng shui
Feng Shui Society
www.fengshuisociety.org.uk

Chapter 2
Choosing your approach

Finding sustainable housing
Commission for Architecture and the Built Environment (CABE)
Homebuyers Guide
www.thehomebuyersguide.org

Greener Living Homes
www.greenerlivinghomes.co.uk

Sherwood Energy Village (SEV)
Info@sev.org.uk

Natural Homes for Sale
www.NaturalHomes-fsbo.com

Urbane
Urban.e@btopenworld.com

Walter Segal Self Build Trust
www.segalselfbuild.co.uk

Cohousing
www.cohousing.co.uk
www.cohousing.org

Ecovillages
www.ecovillage.org
www.ic.org/laev
www.ecovillagefindhorn.com
www.city.davis.ca.us
www.thefarm.org

Sustainable communities
www.sustainable.org
www.hockerton.demon.co.uk
www.segalselfbuild.co.uk
www.bioregional.com

Chapter 3
Getting started

Planning guidance
Royal Town Planning Institute
www.rtpi.org.uk

American Planning Association
www.planning.org

Kit homes
Deltec Homes
www.deltechomes.com

Benfield
www.benfieldatt.co.uk

Log homes
Log-Craft
www.logcraft.co.uk

Log House Builder's Association Of North America
www.premier1.net/~log-house/

Packages
See Earthship

Self-build
www.selfbuildanddesign.com
www.segalselfbuild.co.uk

Self-build courses
Centre of Alternative Technology
courses@cat.org.uk

California Earth Art and Architecture Institute (Cal-Earth)
www.calearth.org

The Canelo Project
www.caneloproject.org

Real Goods Institute for Solar Living
www.solarliving.org
Groundworks
www.cpros.com/-sequoia/workshop.html

Shenoa Retreat and Learning Center
(001) 707 895 3156

Finding a site
Association of Eco-Conscious Builders
www.aecb.net

Sponge network
www.spongenet.org

Finding an architect
Royal Institute of British Architects (RIBA)
www.architecture.com (and for regional offices and branches)

Royal Incorporation of Architects in Scotland (RIAS)
www.rias.org.uk

Royal Society of Ulster Architects (RSUA)
www.rsua.org.uk

Royal Society of Architects in Wales (RSAW)
www.architecture-wales.com

American Institute of Architects (AIA)
www.aia.org (and for local Chapters)

Architects/Designers/Planners for Social Responsibility (ADPSR)
National Forum
http://adpsr.org/ (and for local Chapters)

Finding a builder
Association of Environment Conscious Builders (AECB)
www.aecb.net
(professional and trade members by region)

The Green Register
of Construction Professionals (TGR)
www.greenregister.org

Builders without Borders
www.builderswithoutborders.org

Portland Natural Building Convergence
www.barnit.com

Chapter 4
Creating your design

Design process (general and professional sites)

See RIBA and AIA sites for procedures and types of contracts

Building Research Establishment Environmental Assessment Method (BREEAM)
www.bre.co.uk/services/Sustainable_construction.html
see also "Envest" software

BRE EcoHomes
www.bre.co.uk/ecohomes

Standard Assessment Procedure (SAP)
http://projects.bre.co.uk/sap2001/

National House Building Council (NHBC)
EcoHomes
www.nhbc.co.uk

Solacalc
www.solacalc.freeserve.co.uk

Sustainability Works
(online software for professionals)
www.sustainabilityworks.org.uk

Healthy Home Designs
www.NaturalHomePlans.com

National Green Building Council
www.usgbc.org
(LEED green building rating system)

Green stores/suppliers
Construction Resources
www.ecoconstruct.com

The Green Shop
www.greenshop.co.uk

Green Building Store
www.greenbuildingstore.co.uk

Specifications
GreenSpec
www.greenspec.co.uk

National Building Specification
www.theNBS.com

Timber framing
Timber Framers Guild
www.tfguild.org

Carpenter Oak
www.carpenteroak.com

Ethical funding organizations
Co-operative Bank
www.co-operativebank.co.uk

Triodos Bank
www.triodos.co.uk

Ecology Building Society
www.ecology.co.uk

Chapter 5
Building it

US building codes
International Code Council (ICC)
www.ICCSAFE.org

International Council of Building Officials
www.ICBO.org

Building sustainability code development
Development Center for Appropriate Technology (DCAT)
www.DCAT.net

Ecological Building Network (EBNet)
www.EcoBuildNetwork.org

EcoConstruction
www.ecoconstruction.org

Building courses
Square One
www.squ1.com

Site safety
Considerate Constructors Scheme
www.ccscheme.org.uk

Chapter 6
Designing with natural systems

DEFRA – Sustainable Energy
www.defra.gov.uk/environment/energy/index.htm

Renewable Energy
www.dti.gov.uk/renewable/

Home Power
www.homepower.com

Degree Days
http://vesma.com/ddd/

US Environmental Protection Agency's "Energy Star Program"
www.EnergyStar.gov

American Solar Energy Society
www.ases.org

Center for Renewable Energy and Sustainable Technologies
www.crest.org

Sustainable Buildings Industry Council
www.sbicouncil.org
Real Goods Solar Living Institute
www.solarliving.org

National Energy Foundation
www.greenenergy.org.uk

Centre of Alternative Technology (CAT)
www.cat.org.uk

Powergen "WhisperGen" micro combined heat and power system
www.powergen.co.uk

California Energy Commission
"Cool Savings with Cool Roofs Program"
www.coolroofs.info

Photovoltaics (PV)
Gaiam Real Goods
www.realgoods.com

DTI "Clear Skies Initiative" grants
www.clear-skies.co.uk/
www.clear-skies.org

Solar Electricity
www.solar-power-answers.co.uk

British Photovoltaic Association
www.pv-uk.org.uk/technology

Solar slates
www.solexenergy.co.uk

Green electricity
Save Money on your Gas & Electricity
http://212.241.173.29/greenpower/domestic-inout.asp

Heat-recovery ventilators (HRVs)
Home Ventilating Institute
www.hvi.org

Positive Energy Conservation Products
www.positive-energy.com

Rainwater saving
Rainharvesting Systems
www.rainharvesting.co.uk
www.grow.arizona.edu/

Freerain
www.freerain.co.uk

Solar hot water
www.thecei.org.uk/solarheating/default
.htm

Solartwin
www.solartwin.com

Radiant floor heating
Radiant Floor Company
www.radiantcompany.com

Hydropower
British Hydropower Association
www.british-hydro.org

Wind power
British Wind Energy Association
www.bwea.com

Hugh Piggott's windpower website
www.scoraigwind.com

Wind data
www.winddata.com

Danish Wind Energy Association
www.windpower.dk

Wood stoves
British Biogen
www.Britishbiogen.co.uk

Ceramic Stoves
www.ceramicstove.com

Beacon Stoves
www.beconstoves.co.uk

Tulikivi Soapstone stoves
www.tulikivi.com

Wood fuels
www.woodfuel.com
www.british-pellet-club.org.uk
www.organicenergy.co.uk

Chapter 7
Green building options

Energy and Environmental Building
Association
www.EEBA.org

National Association of the Remodeling
Industry
www.NARI.org

Green Concepts
www.GreenConcepts.com

NAHB Remodelers Council
www.RemodelingResource.com

Salvo
(reclaimed building materials directory)
www.salvo.co.uk

GreenPro
(building product database)
www.newbuilder.co.uk

Insulation
Sheep's wool
www.secondnatureuk.com
www.sheepwoolinsulation.ie
www.ochre-wool.co.uk

Cellulose
www.excelfibre.com
www.celbar.com

**Green building materials/products
suppliers**
National Building Technologies (NBT)
www.naturalbuildingproductscouk.ntite
mp.com

Green Building Store
www.greenbuildingstore.co.uk

Construction Resources
www.ecoconstruct.com

Healthy Home
www.HealthyHome.com

Straw bale
Straw Bale Building Association
www.strawbalebuildingassociation.org.
uk

Amazon Nails
www.strawbalefutures.org

The Last Straw
www.strawhomes.com

Straw-clay
The Econest Building Company
www.econest.com

Earth building
Centre for Earthen Architecture
www.tech.plym.ac.uk/soa/arch/earth.h
tm

CRATerre
www.craterre.archi.fr

Rammed Earth Works
Rew@l-café.net

Cob
Devon Earth Building Association
www.devonearthbuilding.co.uk

The Cob Cottage Company
http://deatech.com/cobcottage

Sustainable wood
The Forest Stewardship Council (FSC)
www.fsc-uk.info

Friends of the Earth "Good Wood
Guide"
www.goodwoodguide.com

Soil Association "Woodmark"
www.soilassociation.org

"Smart Wood" Certification Program
www.smartwood.org

The Timber Research
and Development Association (TRADA)
www.trada.co.uk

Timber-framing
Timber Framers Guild
www.tfguild.org

The Segal Method
www.segalselfbuild.co.uk

Prefabricated walling systems
"Rastra"
Rastra.net
www.greendepotinc.com

New-build wall and roof systems
www.naturalbuildingproductscouk.ntite
mp.com

Green roofs
www.greenroof.co.uk
www.erisco-bauder.co.uk
www.xco2.com

Building with waste
See Earthship

The Materials Information Exchange
(MIE)
www.salvomie.co.uk

Chapter 8
Choosing interior materials
– walls, windows, and
doors

**Natural paints, stains,
and adhesives**
Auro Paints
www.auro.co.uk

Holkham Linseed Paints
www.holkhamlinseedpaints.co.uk

Green Paints
www.greenshop.co.uk

Earth Born
www.earthbornpaints.co.uk

Nutshell Paints
www.nutshellpaints.com

OSMO UK Ltd
www.osmouk.com

AFM Safecoat
www.afmsafecoat.com

Bioshield Paints
www.bioshieldpaint.com

OS Products
www.enviresource.com

Milk Paint
www.milkpaint.com

Livos
www.thenaturalfinish.com

Earth plasters
American Clay
www.americanclay.com

Clay finish
www.constructionresources.com/prod-
ucts/Tierrafino.htm

Lime
www.lime.org.uk
www.virginialimeworks.com

Wall tiles
Geostone Eco-Cycle
www.crossville-ceramics.com

Recycled glass tiles
www.sandhillind.com

Windows
The Swedish Window Company
www.swedishwindows.com

SunPipe Natural Daylight Systems
Windcatcher Natural Ventilation
Systems
www.moondraught.com

Chapter 9
Choosing interior
materials – floors

Healthy Flooring Network
www.healthyflooring.org

Natural carpets
www.earthweave.com
www.NaturesCarpet.com
www.woolshire.com

Linoleum
www.themarmoleumstore.com
www.forbo-linoleum.com

Cork
www.NaturalCork.com

Natural floors
www.planetearth.com
www.naturalhomeproducts.com

Bamboo flooring
www.bamboo-flooring.com
www.sustainableflooring.com
www.ecotimber.com
www.misugidesigns.com

Chapter 10
Personal style and
decoration

Environmental labelling
European Union Energy Label
www.leeac.org.uk

Green Seal
www.greenseal.org

Fair Trade
www.fairtrade.org.uk
www.onevillage.org

Living spaces
Natural Collection
www.naturalcollection.com

Chemical-free upholstered sofas etc
www.furnature.com

Chemical-free fabrics
www.homespunfabrics.com

Natural Window Fashions
www.earthshade.com

Sleeping spaces
Natural beds and bedding
www.alphabeds.co.uk
www.H3Environmental.com
www.SuiteSleep.com
www.samina.com
www.gaiam.com
www.obasan.ca
www.miraorganics.com

Gauss meters (to measure EMFs)
www.LessEMF.com
www.BuildingBiology.net

Cooking and dining spaces
Energy rating of appliances
www.EnergyStar.org

Bathing spaces
Japanese-style soaking baths
www.thgusa.com

Condensing boilers/Tankless Water
Heaters
www.tanklesswaterheaters.com

Waterless Urinals
www.dutavit.com

Low-flush and Composting Toilets
www.rainwaterharvesting.co.uk
www.EcoTechusa.com
www.caromausa.com
www.totousa.com

Low-flow showerheads
and bathroom accessories
www.realgoods.com

Waterfree Technologies
www.falconwaterfree.com

Greywater heat exchangers
www.gfxtechnology.com

Non-toxic household cleaners
www.ecover.com
www.rochestermidland.com
www.seventhgeneration.com

Nature spaces
National Wildlife Federation
"Backyard Wildlife Habitat Program"
www.nwf.org

LifeGarden
www.lifegarden.org

Permaculture Association
www.permaculture.co.uk

Magazines
Building for a Future
www.newbuilder.co.uk

Self Build
www.selfbuildanddesign.com

Ethical Consumer
www.ethicalconsumer.co.uk

Resurgence
www.resurgence.org

Green Futures
www.ForumforFuture.co.uk

Natural Home and Garden Magazine
www.NaturalHomeAndGarden.com

Environmental Building News (EBN)
www.BuildingGreen.com

The Last Straw
www.strawhouses.com

The Permaculture Activist
www.permacultureactivist.net

Joiner's Quarterly
www.foxmaple.com

Specialist bookshops
The Building Centre Bookshop
www.buildingcentre.co.uk

RIBA Bookshops
www.ribabookshops.com

Builders Bookstore
www.BuildersBookstore.com

INDEX

ACKNOWLEDGEMENTS AND CREDITS

Author's acknowledgements

First and foremost, I'd like to thank all the owners and architects of the featured houses for their inspiration, courtesy, and hospitality, and for sparing time from their busy schedules to answer all my queries. Many thanks to Robyn at Natural Home and Garden Magazine *for her initial help in suggesting projects and to the Architects, Designers and Planners for Social Responsibility (ADPSR) for allowing me to invite participation from their members via their website. Also, thanks to all the staff at the Earthship Community for a pleasant stay and to David, Sarah, and James at Springfield Cohousing for their time and assistance.*

My special thanks to the Gaia Books team – Lucy for her creative graphic design and sensitive picture selection, Jonathan for his calm and professional editorial expertise, and to Patrick for his supportive and helpful direction. And lastly, to Joss for setting the book in motion, and all her invaluable assistance and companionship along the way.

Photographic credits

All photographs by David Pearson, except the following: p. 12(below) Michael Kauffman; pp. 14, 15, 16, 17, 18, 19 Stuart Bish; p. 27 Barbara Bourne; pp. 28, 31 Steve Solinsky; pp. 35, 41(below), 43, 44, 45 Steve Teague; pp. 49, 52, 53 Dave Adams, © www.daveadamsphotography.com; pp. 77, 78(below left), 79 Karl Wanaselja; pp 86–7, 91, 119(top), 131(below) Michael Kauffman; pp. 126, 127, 130, 131(top), 132 Karl Wanaselja; p. 137 Barbara Bourne.